KT-527-352

Hasan.

# EU LAW

Dr. Ewan Kirk

**PEARSON**

Longman

Harlow, England • London • New York • Boston • San Francisco • Toronto • Sydney • Singapore • Hong Kong
Tokyo • Seoul • Taipei • New Delhi • Cape Town • Madrid • Mexico City • Amsterdam • Munich • Paris • Milan

*Pearson Education Limited*
Edinburgh Gate
Harlow
Essex CM20 2JE
England

and Associated Companies throughout the

*Visit us on the World Wide Web at:*
www.pearsoned.co.uk

**First published 2009**

© Pearson Education Limited 2009

| LONDON BOROUGH OF WANDSWORTH | |
| --- | --- |
| 9030 00000 0412 3 | |
| Askews | 19-Feb-2009 |
| 341.2422 KIRK | £10.99 |
| | WWX0004383/0002 |

The right of Ewan Kirk to be identified as author of this work
accordance with the Copyright, Designs and Patents Act 1988.

All rights reserved. No part of this publication may be reproduced, stored in a retrieval system,
or transmitted in any form or by any means, electronic, mechanical, photocopying, recording or
otherwise, without either the prior written permission of the publisher or a licence permitting
restricted copying in the United Kingdom issued by the Copyright Licensing Agency Ltd, Saffron
House, 6–10 Kirby Street, London EC1N 8TS.

All trademarks used herein are the property of their respective owners. The use of any
trademark in this text does not vest in the author or publisher any trademark ownership rights
in such trademarks, nor does the use of such trademarks imply any affiliation with or
endorsement of this book by such owners.

Crown Copyright material is reproduced with the permission of the Controller of HMSO and the
Queen's Printer for Scotland.
Law Commission Reports are reproduced under the terms of the Click-Use Licence.

ISBN: 978-1-4058-2193-3

**British Library Cataloguing-in-Publication Data**
A catalogue record for this book is available from the British Library

**Library of Congress Cataloging-in-Publication Data**
Kirk, Ewan.
  EU law / Ewan Kirk. -- 1st ed.
    p. cm. -- (Law express)
  Includes bibliographical references and index.
  ISBN 978-1-4058-2193-3 (alk. paper)
  1. Law--European Union countries. I. Title. II. Title: European Union law.
  KJE947.K57 2008
  341.242'2--dc22

                                                      2008030985

10 9 8 7 6 5 4 3 2 1
13 12 11 10 09

Typeset in 10pt Helvetica by 3
Printed and bound in Great Britain by Henry Ling Ltd, Dorchester, Dorset

*The publisher's policy is to use paper manufactured from sustainable forests.*

# Contents

Acknowledgements                                          vi
Introduction                                              vii
Guided tour                                               x
Guided tour of the companion website                      xii
Table of cases and statutes                               xiv

Chapter 1:   Sources and application of EU law            1
Chapter 2:   The Institutions of the EU                   16
Chapter 3:   Articles 226–228: Enforcement actions against
             Member States                                31
Chapter 4:   Articles 230 and 232: Judicial Review        43
Chapter 5:   Article 234: Preliminary rulings in the ECJ  56
Chapter 6:   Free movement of goods                       73
Chapter 7:   Free movement of workers                     89
Chapter 8:   Competition law                              104

And finally, before the exam ...                          120
Glossary of terms                                         123
Index                                                     125

## Supporting resources

Visit the Law Express Series Companion Website at **www.pearsoned.co.uk/lawexpress** to find valuable student learning material.

### Companion Website for students

- A study plan test to assess how well you know the subject before you begin your revision, now broken down into targeted study units
- Interactive quizzes with a variety of question types to test your knowledge of the main points from each chapter of the book
- Further examination questions and guidelines for answering them
- Interactive flashcards to help you revise the main terms and cases
- Printable versions of the topic maps and checklists
- 'You be the marker' allows you to see exam questions and answers from the perspective of the examiner and includes notes on how an answer might be marked
- Podcasts provide point-by-point instruction on how to answer a common exam question

**Also:** The Companion Website provides the following features:

- Search tool to help locate specific items of content
- E-mail results and profile tools to send results of quizzes to instructors
- Online help and support to assist with website usage and troubleshooting

For more information please contact your local Pearson Education sales representative or visit **www.pearsoned.co.uk/lawexpress**

# Acknowledgements

I'd like to thank all those who helped by reviewing chapters, also Zoe Botterill at Pearson for her continual assistance and support, and her endless, endless patience. Finally and most importantly, Penny.

# Publisher's acknowledgements

Our thanks go to all reviewers who contributed to the development of this text, including students who participated in research and focus groups which helped to shape the series format.

# Introduction

With the rapid development and expansion of the EU, it is becoming more important (if that is possible) for law students to get to grips with EU law. Rules and principles from the EU now affect an ever-expanding list of areas of law as powers are exercised and rules are made by the EU as a whole for the benefit of its Member States.

The EU is also a very different system from the one you will have studied as part of your coursework on the English Legal System. For this reason it appears daunting or 'scary' to many law students. However, this is not the case – EU law is, in some respects, more straightforward than the law in the UK, and a lot more linear. Students often make the mistake of attempting to draw parallels between the English Legal System and the EU system. Although there are some parallels that can be safely drawn, you should not fall into the trap of thinking that the EU is just like the system in the UK – they are very different.

EU law overlaps and connects with other subjects in such a way that it has an effect on just about every area of law you will encounter on a law degree, and therefore it is important to get to grips with the basics of the topic not only for the examinations you will have in this subject, but to help you to gain a better understanding in those other areas.

EU law can be broadly split into two general categories – first there are those aspects that concern the constitutional aspects of EU law, and secondly those that concern substantive elements of EU law (such as competition law, for example).

This book aims to take you through the main areas studied by law students on LL.B degrees in the UK in the area of EU law, both concerning the way in which the EU legal system works, and substantive law subjects. EU law courses vary greatly between institutions, however, so there may be some difference between the content of this book and the syllabus of your course. However, common areas of EU law are covered here, and so you should use this book for what it is – a guide to the main areas in this subject required for you to do well. A word of warning – it is no substitute for your textbooks, your lecture notes and other materials: instead this book should help you to focus in your use of those other materials.

Finally, you should note that this book refers to EU law and Community law throughout, but these are treated as interchangeable terms. The EU is often still referred to (for example in the Treaty of Rome itself) as 'The Community'.

## REVISION NOTES

Things to bear in mind when revising EU law:

▮ EU law is becoming more important as more powers are given to the EU and EU law affects other areas of law

▮ Don't think that the EU is just like the UK legal system – it is very different and has its own rules and traditions

▮ There are legal system and substantive aspects of EU law – make sure you check the syllabus of your course to see where you should focus your study of EU law

▮ Make sure that you make full use of your textbooks and lecture notes in order to understand the subject in depth – this book will not give you everything you need on its own

▮ Make sure you practise essay/problem questions, and get feedback on how you are doing.

# Guided tour

**Topic maps** – Highlight the main points and allow you to find your way quickly and easily through each chapter.

# 1
## Sources and Application of EU Law

**Revision checklist** – how well do you know each topic? Don't panic if you don't know them all, the chapters will help you revise each point so that you will be fully prepared for your exams.

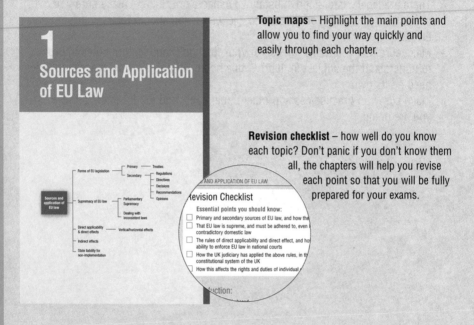

Forms of EU legislation
— Primary — Treaties
— Secondary — Regulations
— Directives
— Decisions
— Recommendations
— Opinions

Sources and application of EU law

Supremacy of EU law
— Parliamentary Supremacy
— Dealing with inconsistent laws

Direct applicability & direct effects — Vertical/horizontal effects

Indirect effects

State liability for non-implementation

... AND APPLICATION OF EU LAW

**Revision Checklist**

Essential points you should know:

☐ Primary and secondary sources of EU law, and how the
☐ That EU law is supreme, and must be adhered to, even i
    contradictory domestic law
☐ The rules of direct applicability and direct effect, and ho
    ability to enforce EU law in national courts
☐ How the UK judiciary has applied the above rules, in th
    constitutional system of the UK
☐ How this affects the rights and duties of individual

duction:

---

**Sample questions** – Prepare for what you will be faced with in your exams! Guidance on structuring strong answers is provided at the end of the chapter.

## Sample question

Could you answer this question? Below is a typical essay question that could arise on this topic. Guidelines on answering the question are included at the end of this chapter, whilst a sample problem question and guidance on tackling it can be found on the companion website.

### Essay question

'... it has become common to speak of an 'institutional balance' within Community institutions, and the way in which this is evoked draws on a system of checks and balances not dissimilar to those we find in more traditional governmental systems. The EU institutions have come to operate a system of checks on each other, sometimes referred to in the context of an "institutional balance" ...'

Douglass-Scott, S., *Constitutional Law of the European Union*, (Longman 2002), Chapter 2 at p.49).

To what extent does the above statement apply to the current relationship between the Commission, the Council of Ministers and the European Parliament, particularly as regards maintaining the balance of interests between the European Union and the Member States?

---

**Key definition boxes** – Make sure you understand essential legal terms.

### KEY DEFINITIONS

**Vertical/horizontal effect** A Community law is vertically effective when it is enforceable only against the State. It is horizontally effective when it is enforceable against private individuals (people and companies).

**Problem area** – Highlight areas where students most often trip up in exams. Use them to make sure you do not make the same mistakes.

**Key case and key statute boxes** – Identify the essential cases and statutes that you need to know for your exams.

**Further thinking box** – Illustrates areas of academic debate, and point you towards that extra reading required for the top grades.

**Glossary – forgotten the meaning of a word?** Where a word is highlighted in the text, turn to the glossary at the back of the book to remind yourself of its meaning.

**Exam tips** – Want to impress examiners? These indicate how you can improve your exam performance and your chances of getting top marks.

**Revision notes** – Highlight points that you should be aware of in other topic areas, or where your course may adopt a specific approach that you should check with your course tutor before reading further.

---

**Problem area: Commission discretion**

The important point to make here is the discretion that the Commission has in bringing this procedure. Article 226 says '*IF* the Commission considers that a Member State has failed to fulfil an obligation …' The Commission has a lot of discretion as to when it is going to take action, and for which infringements. Case 247/87 *Star Fruit Company* v. *Commission* (1989) ECR 291 shows that the Commission can't be forced to take action under Article 226.

There is also no time limit on the different actions of the Commission under the Administrative Stage, and so they can take the next step in the process when they wish, if at all. About 90% of all Article 226 actions are resolved in this stage without going to the ECJ, and the way in which the Commission manages these situations is part of this.

You should bear in mind that as a result an individual cannot force the Commission to take action, but a Member State can take action itself under Article 227. An individual is better off trying to use Direct Effects against the Member State. When revising this subject, remember there are alternatives, and that this procedure is part of a wider system. This can be an important point to remember in a problem question such as the one at the beginning of this chapter, but also in an essay question about the Commission's discretion in Article 226.

**KEY STATUTE**

**Article 227(1)**

A Member State which considers that another Member State has failed to fulfil an obligation under this Treaty may bring the matter before the Court of Justice.

**KEY CASE**

*R* v. *Secretary of State for* 3 CMLR 1

**Concerning: supremacy of EU**

Facts

A dispute arose over the Mercha restrict ownership of UK registe 75% of the boat must be own there was a direct conflict b Treaty, which should be a

**FURTHER THINKING**

Commission discretion is an important part of the flexibility of the Article 226 procedure – the Commission makes its own decisions as to which actions to pursue, but at the same time it means it can go after the more serious infringements first. For further reading on this, see Evans, A. (1979) 'The Enforcement Procedure of Article 169 EEC: Commission Discretion'. (Article 169 is the old numbering for Article 226.)

# Glossary of terms

The glossary is divided into two parts: **key definitions** and **other useful terms**. The **key definitions** can be found within the chapter in which they occur as well as at the end of the book. These definitions are the essential terms that you must know and understand in order to prepare for an exam.

The additional list, **other useful terms** provides further definitions of useful terms and phrases which will also help you answer examination and coursework questions effectively. These terms are highlighted in the text as they occur but the definition can only be found here.

## ▌Key definitions

| | |
|---|---|
| *Acte clair* | A condition under which an issue of EU law is clear and does not need to be clarified by the ECJ |
| Court of last instance | In a court structure, this is the very last or highest court that a particular case can reach |
| Court or tribunal | Generally a court or tribunal is one that has a judicial function, and independence from the parties concerned |

**EXAM TIP**

Although the Commission is still involved in Article 227, the thing to remember is that they are not able to delay or dictate the timing of the action taken here. This may be important if the Commission refused to take action themselves under Article 226. It is also important to remember this if you are being asked to advise a Member State in a problem question.

**REVISION NOTE**

Only secondary sources of law are dealt with by this area of the Treaty – Treaty Articles themselves cannot be challenged. See Chapter 2 for a fuller examination of those sources of law. In this chapter, where it refers to a 'Community Act', then it concerns these secondary sources of law.

# Guided tour for companion website

 Book resources are available to download. Print your own **topic maps** and **revision checklists!**

 Use the **study plan** prior to your revision to help you assess how well you know the subject and determine which areas need most attention. Choose to take the full assessment or focus on targeted study units.

 **'Test your knowledge'** of individual areas with quizzes tailored specifically to each chapter. A variety of multiple choice, true and false and fill-in-the-blank question types ensure you are prepared for anything. Sample problem and essay questions are also available with guidance on crafting a good answer.

 **Flashcards** help improve recall of important legal terms and key cases. Use online, print for a handy reference or download to iPod for on-the-go revision!

**'You be the marker'** gives you the chance to evaluate sample exam answers for different question types and understand how and why an examiner awards marks.

Download the **podcast** and listen as your own personal Law Express tutor guides you through a 10-15 minute audio session. You will be presented with a typical but challenging question and provided a step-by-step explanation on how to approach the question, what essential elements your answer will need for a pass, how to structure a good response, and what to do to make your answer stand out so that you can earn extra marks.

All of this and more can be found when you visit
**www.pearsoned.co.uk/lawexpress**

# Table of cases and statutes

## ■UK cases

*Arsenal Football Club* v. *Reed* [2001] 2 CMLR 23 59, 60, 62, 69

*B&I Line* v. *Sealink Harbours & Stena Sealink* (1992) 5 CMLR 255 114

*Bulmer* v. *Bollinger* (1974) Ch 401 66

*Commissioners of Customs & Excise* v. *Samex ApS* (1983) 3 CMLR 194 65

*Hagen* v. *Fratelli* (1980) 3 CMLR 253 66

*Macarthys* v. *Smith* (1979) 3 All ER 325 6

*NUT* v. *Governing Body of St. Mary's Church of England (Aided) Junior School* (1997) 3 CMLR 630 11

*R* v. *Henn & Darby* [1978] 1 WLR 1031 69

*R* v. *Secretary of State for Transport, ex parte Factortame (No.2)* (1990) 3 CMLR 1 7, 13

*Rolls Royce* v. *Doughty* (1992) ICR 538 11

*Wellingborough Borough Council* v. *Payless DIY Ltd* (1990) 1 CMLR 773 83

## ■EU cases

*AITEC* v. *Commission*, Case T-447-449/93 (1995) ECR II-1971 49, 54

*Belgium* v. *Spain*, Case C-388/95 (2000) ECR I-3123 39

*Bonsignore* v. *Oberstadtdirektor of the City of Cologne*, Case 67/74 (1975) ECR 297 100

*Brasserie de Haecht* v. *Wilkin*, Case 23/67 (1967) ECR 407 111

*Brasserie du Pecheur* v. *Germany*, Case C-46/93 [1996] 1 CMLR 889 13

*Brian Francis Collins* v. *Secretary of State for Work and Pensions*, Case C-138/02 (2004) ECR I-2703 95

*British Airways* v. *Commission*, Case T-219/99 (2004) All ER (EC) 1115 115, 116

*British Leyland* v. *Commission*, Case 226/84 (1986) ECR 3263 116

*Broekmeulen* v. *Huisarts Registratie Commissie*, Case 246/80 [1981] ECR 2311 63

*Campus Oil Ltd* v. *Minister for Industry*, Case 72/83 [1984] ECR 2727 86

*CILFIT and Others* v. *Ministro della Sanità*, Case 283/81 (1982) ECR 3415 67

*Cinétheque SA* v. *Fédération Nationale des Cinémas Françaises*, Cases 60 & 61/84 (1985) ECR 2605 80

*Codorniu* v. *EC Council*, Case C-309/89 (1994) ECR I-1853 49

*Commission* v. *Belgium*, Case 77/69 (1970) ECR 237 **34**

*Commission* v. *Germany (Beer Purity Laws)*, Case 178/84 (1987) ECR 1227 **81**

*Commission* v. *Greece*, Case C-240/86 (1988) ECR 1835 **37**

*Conegate* v. *Customs & Excise*, Case 121/85 [1986] ECR 1007 **86**

*Consten* v. *Commission*, Case 56&58/64 (1966) ECR 299 **110**

*Costa* v. *ENEL*, Case 6/64 [1964] ECR 585 **61, 66**

*Criminal Proceedings Against Prantl*, Case 16/83 (1984) ECR 1299 **81**

*Da Costa en Schaake NV* v. *Nederlandse Belastingadministratie*, Case 28-30/62 (1963) ECR 31 **68**

*Defrenne* v. *SABENA (No.2)*, Case 43/75 (1979) ECR 1365 **10**

*Deutsche Grammophon Gesellschaft mbH* v. *Metro-SB-Grossmarkte GmbH*, Case 78/70 (1971) ECR 487 **86**

*EC Commission* v. *Denmark*, Case 302/86 (1988) ECR 4607 **80**

*Eridana* v. *Commission*, Case 10 & 18/68 (1969) ECR 459 **50**

*European Parliament* v. *Commission*, Case 13-83 (1985) ECR 1513 **52**

*Foglia* v. *Novello (No.2)*, Case 244/80 (1981) ECR 3045 **61**

*Foster* v. *British Gas*, Case C-188/89 (1990) ECR I-3313 **10**

*France* v. *Commission*, Case C-327/91 (1994) ECR I-3641 **51**

*France* v. *UK*, Case 141/78 (1979) ECR 2923 **39**

*Francovich* v. *Italy*, Case C-6&9/90 (1991) ECR I-5357 **13**

*Franz Grad* v. *Finanzamt Traustein*, Case 9/70 (1970) ECR 825 **3**

*Hoekstra* v. *BBDA*, Case 75/63 (1964) ECR 177 **94**

*Hoffman la Roche* v. *Commission*, Case 85/76 (1979) ECR 1869 **115, 116**

*Hünermund*, Case C-292/92 [1993] ECR 1-6787 **82**

*International Fruit Co.* v. *Commission*, Case 41-44/70 (1971) ECR 411 **48**

*Italy* v. *EC Council*, Case 166/78 (1979) ECR 2575 **47**

*Keck & Mithouard*, Cases C-267 & C-268/91 (1993) ECR 1-6097 **82**

*Kempf* v. *Staatssecretaris van Justitie*, Case 139/85 (1986) ECR 1741 **93**

*KSH* v. *Intervention Board*, Case 101/76 (1977) ECR 797 **51**

*Lawrie-Blum* v. *Land Baden-Württemburg*, Case 66/85 (1986) ECR 2121 **93, 94**

*Leclerc-Siplec* v. *TF1 Publicité SA*, Case C-412/93 [1995] ECR 179 **82**

*'Les Verts'* v. *Parliament*, Case 294/83 (1986) ECR 1339 **49**

*Levin* v. *Staatssecretaris van Justitie*, Case 53/81 (1982) ECR 1035 **93**

*Lord Bethel* v. *Commission*, Case 246/81 (1982) ECR 2277 **52**

*Maizena* v. *Council*, Case 139/79 (1980) ECR 3393 **51**

*Marleasing* v. *La Comercial Internacional de Alimentación*, Case C-106/89 (1990) ECR I-4135 **11**

*Marshall* v. *Southampton & South West Hampshire Area Health Authority*, Case 152/84 (1986) ECR 723 **10, 11**

*Nordsee Hochseefischerei GmbH*, Case 102/81 [1982] ECR 1095 **64**

*Plaumann* v. *Commission*, Case 25/62 (1963) ECR 95 **49**

*Procureur du Roi* v. *Dassonville*, Case 8/74 (1974) ECR 837 **78**

*Pubblico Ministero* v. *Ratti*, Case 148/78 (1979) ECR 1629 **10**

*R* v. *Bouchereau*, Case 30/77 (1977) ECR 1999 **98, 100**

R v. Immigration Appeal Tribunal ex
parte Antonissen, Case C-292/89
(1991) ECR I-745 94
R v. Secretary of State for Transport, ex
parte Factortame, Case C-48/93 (1996)
ECR I-1029 13
R v. Thompson, Case 7/78 [1978] ECR
2247, [1979] I CMLR 47 86
Radio Telefis Eireann v. Commission,
Case T-70/89 (1991) ECR II-485 116
Re Export Tax on Art Treasures: EC
Commission v. Italy, Case 7/68 (1968)
ECR 423 at 428 76, 86
Re Jules Borker, Case 138/80 [1980]
ECR 1975 64
Re: Tachographs (Commission v. UK),
Case 128/78 (1979) ECR 419 37
Rewe-Zentral AG v.
Bundesmonopolverwaltung für
Branntwein (Cassis de Dijon), Case
120/78 (1979) ECR 649 75, 79, 80, 81
Rewe-Zentralfinanz GmbH v.
Landwirtschaftskammer, Case 4/75
(1975) ECR 843 86
Salgoil SA v. Italian Minister of Foreign
Trade, Case 13/68 (1968) ECR 453 61
Schwarz v. Burgermeister Salzburg, Case
C-366/04 [2005] ECR 1-10139 82
Sofrimport v. Commission, Case 152/88
[1990] ECR 1-2477 54
Spain v. UK, Case C-145/04 (2006) ECR
I-7917 39
Star Fruit Company v. Commission, Case
247/87 (1989) ECR 291 36
Steymann v. Staatssecretaris van Justitie,
Case 196/87 (1988) ECR 6159 93
Stichtig Greenpeace v. Commission, Case
T-585/93 (1995) ECR II-2205 49, 54
Stoke-on-Trent City Council v. B&Q Plc,
Case C-169/91 (1992) ECR I-6635 80,
83
Suiker Unie v. Commission, Case 11, 40-8,
50, 56, 113-4/73 (1975) ECR 1663 109

Terres Rouges Consultant v. EC
Commission, Case T-47/95 (1997)
ECR II-481 50
Tetra-Pak v. Commission, Case T-83/91
(1994) ECR II-755 114
Torfaen Borough Council v. B&Q Plc,
Case C-145/88 (1989) ECR 3851 83
United Brands v. Commission, Case
27/76 (1978) ECR 207 114, 115
van Duyn v. Home Office, Case 41/74
(1974) ECR 1337 9, 98, 99
van Gend en Loos v. Nederlandse
Administratie der Belastingen, Case
26/62 (1963) ECR 1 6, 8, 77
Vereingegen Unwesen in Handel v. Mars
GmbH, Case C-470/93 [1995] ECR
1-1923 82
Volk v. Vervaecke, Case 5/69 (1969) ECR
295 111
Volvo v. Eric Veng, Case 238/87 (1988)
ECR 6211 116
von Colson v. Land Nordrhein-Westfalen,
Case 14/83 (1984) ECR 1891 12
Walter Rau Lebensmittelwerke v. De
Smedt PVBA, Case 261/81 (1982) ECR
3961 79, 81

## Statutes

European Communities Act 1972, c.68 5
European Community Treaty (Treaty of
Rome) 1957
Article 10 5, 35
Article 23 75
Article 25 76
Article 28 76, 77
Article 29 76, 83
Article 30 76, 85
Article 39 92, 95, 96
Article 81 106
Article 82 113, 115
Article 201 25

Article 213 **21**
Article 214(2) **25**
Article 226 **34**
Article 227 **37**
Article 228 **37, 39**
Article 230 **25, 45, 47, 48, 50**
Article 232 **25, 51, 52**
Article 234 **59, 64, 65**
Article 242 **40**

Article 243 **40**
Article 249 **4**
Article 251 **24**
Article 252 **24**
Directive 70/50/EEC **78**
Directive 2004/38/EC **90, 92, 94, 96, 97, 98, 99**
Regulation 1/2003/EC **118**
Regulation 1612/68/EEC **92, 96**

# 1

# Sources and application of EU law

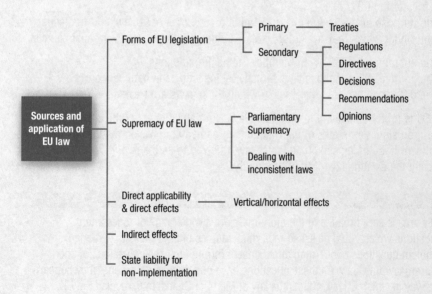

- Forms of EU legislation
  - Primary —— Treaties
  - Secondary
    - Regulations
    - Directives
    - Decisions
    - Recommendations
    - Opinions

**Sources and application of EU law**

- Supremacy of EU law
  - Parliamentary Supremacy
  - Dealing with inconsistent laws

- Direct applicability & direct effects —— Vertical/horizontal effects

- Indirect effects

- State liability for non-implementation

A printable version of this topic map is available from www.pearsoned.co.uk/lawexpress

# Revision Checklist

## Essential points you should know:

- [ ] Primary and secondary sources of EU law, and how they are created
- [ ] That EU law is supreme, and must be adhered to, even in the light of contradictory domestic law
- [ ] The rules of direct applicability and direct effect, and how they affect the ability to enforce EU law in national courts
- [ ] How the UK judiciary has applied the above rules, in the light of the constitutional system of the UK
- [ ] How this affects the rights and duties of individual citizens.

# Introduction:

The operation of the EU is based upon its laws. These laws are created, either through amendments to the Treaties, or through the legislative powers given to the Institutions (see Chapter 2), and are, to a greater or lesser extent, enforceable in or against the countries of the EU.

The purpose of this chapter is to examine the sources of EU law, and to discuss the system under which they are enforceable. To this end, there are several main issues:

- The supremacy of EU law in Member States' jurisdictions
- The enforceability of those laws directly by individuals in national courts
- The difference between the ways in which those laws are treated.

The EU is pretty unusual in international law. Normally it is very difficult to enforce laws upon signatory states of international agreements; however, the EU has built up a significant body of legislation and case law, referred to as the *acquis communitaire* – basically the existing law of the Community.

---

### Assessment advice

This area is very broad, and therefore there are a wide range of assessment questions which could be asked regarding sources of law. These may range from problem questions concerning direct effects through to essay questions on the supremacy of EU law. All these questions have one thing in common – they concern the way in which EU law affects the law of Member States; in particular, the UK.

This is an area of law that has been developed through the case law. It is very important to make sure you are familiar with the key cases that have developed the law here. Examiners will not mark you very highly if you cannot demonstrate a good knowledge of relevant key cases. This chapter will aim to highlight a lot of those cases.

## Sample question

Could you answer this question? Below is a typical essay question that could arise on this topic. Guidelines on answering the question are included at the end of this chapter, whilst a sample problem question and guidance on tackling it can be found on the companion website.

### Essay question

'It is true that by Article 249 [formerly Article 189] regulations are directly applicable and may therefore certainly produce direct effects by virtue of their nature as law. However, it does not follow from this that other categories of legal measures mentioned in that Article could never produce similar effects.'

Case 9/70 *Franz Grad* v. *Finanzamt Traustein* (1970) ECR 825 at 837

**Discuss.**

# ■ Forms of EU legislation

EU Law falls broadly into two categories, primary legislation and secondary legislation:

▌ Primary legislation comes from the Treaties
▌ Secondary legislation comes from the law-making powers given to the Institutions under Article 249.

## Primary legislation

### Problem area: Treaties

There are now a range of Treaties that affect EU law. However, their place is easy to understand as follows:

▌ The Treaty of Rome is the founding treaty of the European Economic Community (now European Community) and is the main treaty to refer to. Where this book refers to 'the Treaty', then it is this treaty which is meant.
▌ The Single European Act, Maastricht Treaty (Treaty on European Union), Amsterdam Treaty, Treaty of Nice and Lisbon Treaty have all amended (or in the case of Lisbon are going to amend) the Treaty of Rome, and therefore commonly you will not need to refer to them directly (with the exception of the Maastricht Treaty which was a more significant amendment than others). Any changes these treaties have made are included in the most up-to-date version of the Treaty of Rome on the Europa website: http://europa.eu/

The order of the Treaties is given in the Table.

| Year | Treaty |
| --- | --- |
| 1957 | Treaty of Rome – EC Treaty |
| 1986 | Single European Act |
| 1992 | Treaty of Maastricht (Treaty on European Union) |
| 1997 | Treaty of Amsterdam |
| 1999 | Treaty of Nice |
| 2007 | Treaty of Lisbon |

Primary legislation is only made when Member States meet and agree amendments; usually at Intergovernmental Conferences. The laws contained in Treaties cannot be changed in any other way, and must do so with the agreement of all Member States.

# Secondary legislation

Secondary legislation is made by the Institutions under the powers given to them by Article 249.

> **KEY STATUTE**
>
> **Article 249(1)**
>
> In order to carry out their task and in accordance with the provisions of this Treaty, the European Parliament acting jointly with the Council, the Council and the Commission shall make regulations and issue directives, take decisions, make recommendations or deliver opinions.

The five different forms of secondary legislation can be defined as follows:

| Form of legislation | Effect |
| --- | --- |
| Regulations (Article 249(2)) | Generally applicable – automatically become law in all Member States |
| Directives (Article 249(3)) | Applicable to all Member States, but require some form of enabling legislation from National Parliaments of Member States |
| Decisions (Article 249(4)) | Binding only on those parties to whom they are addressed |
| Regulations and Opinions (Article 249(5)) | Non-binding Acts |

# ■ Supremacy of EU law

When a Member State joins the EU, they effectively agree to be bound by its laws, both primary and secondary. In particular, Article 10 of the Treaty imposes a general obligation on all Member States to make sure they fulfil all obligations under the Treaty. This created a problem with the UK constitutional system when the UK joined in 1972, as the UK system is dualist.

| KEY DEFINITION |
| --- |

**Dualist** A legal system where any international agreements signed by that State's government can only become law when legislation is enacted in that country to ratify that agreement. This is common in systems where the parliament is supreme, like the UK constitutional system. This is the opposite of monist systems, where any international agreement automatically becomes part of that State's law merely because the government has signed it.

## The Doctrine of Parliamentary Supremacy

The Doctrine of Parliamentary Supremacy creates problems, because it states that:

■ Parliament is the highest law-making body in the UK
■ No other law can override the wishes of Parliament
■ Parliament cannot bind its successors.

This was addressed when the UK joined the EU through Parliament's enactment of the European Communities Act 1972.

**KEY STATUTE**

**European Communities Act 1972**

s.2(1): All rights, powers, liabilities, obligations and restrictions ... arising ... under ... the Treaties are without further enactment to be given legal effect or used in the United Kingdom and shall be recognised and available in law, and be enforced, allowed and followed accordingly ...

Therefore the treaties are recognised as part of UK law because of the European Communities Act, and so this should deal with the issue created by the Doctrine of Parliamentary Supremacy.

## Dealing with inconsistent laws

Joining the EU therefore has two consequences for the UK:

- Any existing national laws inconsistent with EU laws must be repealed
- The Member State must not enact laws in the future which are inconsistent with EU law.

This is due to the fact that, as stated in Case 26/62 *Van Gend en Loos* v. *Nederlandse Administratie der Belastingen* (1963) ECR 1, '... the Community constitutes a new legal order in international law, for whose benefit the States have limited their sovereign rights ...' and therefore limited their ability to make laws which go against the Treaty. The significance of this was discussed by Lord Denning in the following case:

---

**KEY CASE**

*Macarthys* v. *Smith* (1979) 3 All ER 325

**Concerning: the effect of the EC Treaty on the application of UK law in the courts**

Facts

The facts of this case do not aid an understanding of the legal principle.

Legal principle

Lord Denning said:

'In construing our statute, we are entitled to look at the treaty as an aid to its construction: and even more, not only as an aid but as an overriding force. If on close investigation it should appear that our legislation is deficient – or is inconsistent with Community law – by some oversight of our draftsmen – then it is our bounden duty to give priority to Community law.'

---

This is fine where the statute concerned can be reinterpreted, but the principle here was properly tested in the next case.

KEY CASE

**R v. Secretary of State for Transport, ex parte Factortame (No.2) (1990) 3 CMLR 1**

**Concerning: supremacy of EU law and conflicting national law**

Facts

A dispute arose over the Merchant Shipping Act 1988, which attempted to restrict ownership of UK registered fishing boats by requiring that at least 75% of the boat must be owned by UK nationals. The courts had to decide, as there was a direct conflict between the Merchant Shipping Act and the EC Treaty, which should be applied.

Legal principle

After referring this to the ECJ for clarification, the House of Lords decided that where there is conflict between a national law and Community law, that the doctrine of Parliamentary Supremacy is modified by s.2(4) of the European Communities Act 1972, and allowed the House of Lords to disregard the Merchant Shipping Act, something it had never been able to do before. In this case, this allowed the Spanish fishermen who complained to the courts to get interim relief, and eventually led to the relevant parts of the Merchant Shipping Act being repealed.

It is important to point out that this is the case *regardless of whether the Act in question came before or after the European Communities Act.*

# Direct applicability and direct effects

**Problem area:** Direct applicability or direct effect?

There is often confusion between the terms direct applicability and direct effect. It is important not to get these two concepts mixed up as they are quite different. As a general definition, you can think of the two as follows:

**Direct applicability**: EU law is directly applicable if it is recognised as part of UK law. Treaties and Regulations are directly applicable because they become part of UK law as a result of the European Communities Act 1972. Directives are not directly applicable as they need an implementing piece of UK legislation to become law in the UK.

**Directly effective**: EU law is directly effective if it can be enforced in a UK court. There are two types of direct effects, horizontal and vertical. The difference between these two is explained further below.

Linked to the issue of supremacy of Community law is the question of directly enforcing Community law in national courts. The above discussion has shown that Community law overrides UK law, but this is meaningless unless a person can enforce those laws in a UK court. However, in certain circumstances, Community law has been held to be directly enforceable in national courts through the Doctrine of Direct Effects. This was first raised in the following key case.

**KEY CASE**

**Case 26/62 *Van Gend en Loos* v. *Nederlandse Administratie der Belastingen* (1963) ECR 1**

**Concerning: direct effect of Community law in national courts**

Facts

This case concerned Article 25 (formerly Article 12) of the Treaty which prohibited new customs duties being imposed, or existing customs duties being increased. Through a case in the Dutch courts, Van Gend was trying to directly enforce the rule in Article 25 against the Dutch government, claiming it gave them a right not to be taxed in this way. The question was referred to the ECJ under Article 234.

Legal principle

Although Article 25 was a prohibition, the ECJ said that Van Gend could enforce this against the Dutch government if the following criteria were fulfilled:

■ That it was a clear and unconditional prohibition
■ That it imposed a duty without any discretion given to the Member States
■ That it produced direct effects between Member States and citizens.

As these criteria were fulfilled in this case, then the national court could enforce Article 25 in favour of Van Gend.

DIRECT APPLICABILITY AND DIRECT EFFECTS

DIRECT APPLICABILITY AND DIRECT EFFECTS

**KEY CASE**

**Case 41/74 *Van Duyn* v. *Home Office* (1974) ECR 1337**

**Concerning: criteria for establishing whether a provision of Community law has direct effect**

Facts

The UK government was attempting to exclude van Duyn, a Dutch national, from the UK because of her membership of an 'undesirable' organisation, the Church of Scientology. Part of this case looked at whether Directive 64/221 could be directly enforced by van Duyn.

Legal principle

In order for a provision of Community law to have direct effects, it must be:

▪ Clear and precise
▪ Unconditional/without exceptions
▪ Not require any implementation by the Member States.

These cases clearly established that it was possible for an individual to enforce a rule of Community law, without having to rely upon a national rule. The application of this rule, however, will be different according to the different type of Community Act being enforced. Treaties and Regulations are directly applicable and directly effective, but Directives are not directly applicable, and are only directly effective **vertically**.

# Vertical and horizontal effect

**KEY DEFINITION**

**Vertical/horizontal effect** A Community law is **vertically effective** when it is enforceable only against the State. It is **horizontally effective** when it is enforceable against private individuals (people and companies).

| Type of Community law | Vertically/horizontally effective? |
|---|---|
| Treaties | Can be both vertically and horizontally effective, depending on the nature of the right being given by the Treaty article |
| Regulations | Can be both vertically and horizontally effective |
| Directives | Vertically effective only – a directive is an instruction to a State to introduce a law into their own legal system |
| Decisions | Decisions are addressed to particular parties – so they are enforceable only against those parties |

# The problem of direct effect of directives

This is the part of direct effect that students struggle most with – directly enforcing a directive in a national court causes the most problems because of the nature of a directive. Directives are instructions to the Member States to enact a law, and therefore they are only capable of having vertical effect. The main thing to note is that directives do not **automatically** have direct effects, and so if a person wants to enforce them in a national court, they must make sure the following conditions apply.

| Condition | Case example |
|---|---|
| The Directive must give clearly identifiable rights to individuals | Case 43/75 Defrenne v. SABENA (No.2) (1979) ECR 1365 |
| The time limit for the Member State to implement the Directive must have passed | Case 148/78 Pubblico Ministero v. Ratti (1979) ECR 1629 |
| The Directive can be enforced only against the State (vertically) | Case 152/84 Marshall v. Southampton & South West Hampshire Area Health Authority (1986) ECR 723 |

**Problem area:** 'The State'

One area where the ECJ has been flexible with its definition concerns what is 'the State' under the vertical effects rule. This is an area where students can be caught out when dealing with a problem question which involves vertical effect. Look at these three examples:

In Case C-188/89 Foster v. British Gas (1990) ECR I-3313 the ECJ said that a body would be part of the State if it:

■ is subject to the control of the State
■ has special powers given to it by the State.

Case 152/84 *Marshall* v. *Southampton & South West Hampshire Area Health Authority* (1986) ECR 723 shows that 'the State' is 'the State' regardless of what function it is performing (in *Marshall* it was acting as an employer).

In *NUT* v. *Governing Body of St. Mary's Church of England (Aided) Junior School* (1997) 3 CMLR 630 the court decided that the definition of 'the State' should be a 'broad one'. Schools and other educational establishments would therefore be part of 'the State'.

When thinking about whether something is part of 'the State', it is important to bear in mind this broad definition – but there are limits: see *Rolls Royce* v. *Doughty* (1992) ICR 538 where although Rolls Royce were publicly owned, they were not part of 'the State'.

# ■ Other ways of enforcing EU law in national courts

As well as using direct effects, there are other ways in which Directives can be enforced in national courts. These apply to all forms of EU law mentioned in this chapter, but are particularly of relevance to the problem question asked on the companion website.

## Indirect effect

When EU law imposes an obligation on 'the State', the definition is very broad, and therefore also includes the courts as well. This has led to the ECJ finding that the courts also have an obligation to interpret national law in line with EU law:

KEY CASE

**Case 14/83 *von Colson* v. *Land Nordrhein-Westfalen* (1984) ECR 1891**

**Concerning: indirect effect of Community law**

Facts

The facts of this case do not aid an understanding of the legal principle.

Legal principle

The ECJ developed what is often referred to as the 'von Colson principle': that as national courts are part of The State, they are under an obligation to interpret national law in line with Community law. This can mean that an individual can enforce a law from the EU against another individual in a national court.

This appears to solve all problems created by the limits of direct effects (particularly with Directives, because they can only have vertical effects), but if you look at Case C-106/89 *Marleasing* v. *La Comercial Internacional de Alimentación* (1990) ECR I-4135, it is important that a national law *exists* that can be interpreted.

## State liability for non-implementation

There is one final method of gaining a remedy based on EU law – to sue the State because of its failure to implement a piece of legislation where it was obliged to do so. This is **mainly** relevant to Directives, because they normally need a national law to give effect to them, but not exclusively.

KEY CASE

### Case C-6&9/90 *Francovich* v. *Italy* (1991) ECR I-5357

### Concerning: state liability for failing to implement a Directive

#### Facts

This case concerned employees of a bankrupt company who were trying to claim wages arrears, something which was guaranteed by a Directive which Italy had failed to implement. Because they could not sue their former employer (because that would have involved a horizontal effect, not possible with a Directive) they then sued the Italian State, claiming that it was at fault because they could not get a remedy.

#### Legal principle

The ECJ held that the Italian State would be liable for their failure to implement the Directive if the following three conditions were fulfilled:

■ the Directive gave rights to individuals
■ those rights were identifiable within the wording of the Directive
■ there was a causal link between the failure to implement and the damage caused to the individual.

This has now been applied to all forms of Community law (see Cases C-46&48/93 *Brasserie du Pecheur* v. *Germany* and *R* v. *Secretary of State for Transport, ex parte Factortame* (1996) ECR I-1029). These cases also added the principle that the breach must be 'sufficiently serious' in order to be able to apply this principle to all forms of Community law.

### FURTHER THINKING

A more controversial aspect of State Liability has been the idea that the State could be liable for the actions of the judiciary. See Anagnostaras, G. (2001) *The Principle of State Liability for Judicial Breaches: The Impact of European Community Law.*

# Chapter summary:
# Putting it all together

☐ Can you tick all the points from the revision checklist at the beginning of this chapter?

☐ Take the **end-of-chapter quiz** on the companion website.

☐ Test your knowledge of the cases below with the **revision flashcards** on the website.

☐ Attempt the essay question from the beginning of the chapter using the guidelines below.

☐ Go to the companion website to try out other questions.

## Answer guidelines

**See the essay question at the start of the chapter. This question is focused upon the principle of direct effects discussed in part of this chapter, but it is also broad enough to enable you to bring in other areas of this topic from this chapter.**

In your answer, you will need to address the following:

▌ The distinction between direct applicability and direct effect
▌ The different rules for direct applicability/effects of Treaties, Regulations, Directives, Decisions
▌ A discussion of how the rules have been applied by the courts to these different forms of legislation, in particular, the way in which rules concerning Directives have evolved
▌ How the shortcomings of direct effect of Directives (lack of horizontal effect) have been addressed through use of indirect effect and state liability for non-implementation.

### Make your answer stand out

This question is asking you to explain the operation of the rules of direct applicability/effects to forms of legislation other than Regulations, and the most complicated of these is Directives. Directives create problems because of the nature of what they are: instructions to Member States. Therefore if you can show your appreciation of the limitations of Directives, and how the courts have developed rules to deal with this (for example, the broad definition of 'the State' discussed above) as well as the limitations still in existence (the difference in employees in the public and private sector under the rules in *Marshall*, for example) then you can show an appreciation of how these rules work in practice.

## FURTHER READING

Anagnostaras, G. (2001) 'The Principle of State Liability for Judicial Breaches: the Impact of European Community Law', EPL 281

Craig, P. (1991) 'Sovereignty of the United Kingdom Parliament after *Factortame*', 9 YEL 221

Craig, P. (1997) Directives: Direct Effect, Indirect Effect and the Construction of National Legislation', 22 EL Rev 519

Craig, P. (1997) 'Once More Unto the Breach: the Community, the State and Damages Liability', 113 LQR 67

Tridimas, T. (2002) 'Black, White, and Shades of Grey: Horizontality of Directives Revisited', 21 YEL 327

Steiner, J. (1993) 'From Direct Effects to *Francovich*: Shifting Means of Enforcement of Community Law', 18 EL Rev 3

# 2
# The Institutions of the EU

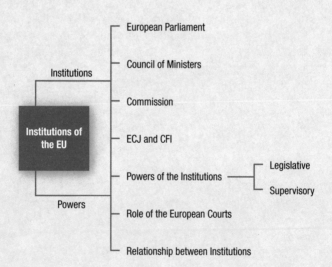

- Institutions
  - European Parliament
  - Council of Ministers
  - Commission
  - ECJ and CFI

**Institutions of the EU**

- Powers
  - Powers of the Institutions
    - Legislative
    - Supervisory
  - Role of the European Courts
  - Relationship between Institutions

A printable version of this topic map is available from www.pearsoned.co.uk/lawexpress

# Revision Checklist

## Essential points you should know:

- [ ] The structure of the EU Institutions and how they relate to each other
- [ ] The role of each of the Institutions, and their powers and duties
- [ ] How the above affects both the political and legal life of the Community, and the implications of the exercise of those powers by the Institutions.

# Introduction:

**The EU is run by its Institutions**. Therefore the key to understanding the way in which the EU operates lies in understanding the functions of the Institutions. The EU has two very important functions which have a very real effect on the Member States. First, it makes law, whether that be through Treaties or secondary legislation, and secondly, it provides adjudication on those laws applicable to all Member States. Each of the Institutions has a key role in achieving these functions, and their powers and their interrelationships are important in showing how this works. The functions and powers of the Institutions tend not to contribute to their own discrete question in an examination, as something focused purely on the mechanics of how the Institutions do things would present a topic purely descriptive in nature. However, an analysis of the politics of how the Institutions work and the political context in which EU law operates can form part of a question in this area. It also helps to understand the Institutions for other topics such as the legislative process itself, and the actions of the three main Institutions when appearing in front of the ECJ. In this chapter we are going to examine the relationships between the Institutions in order to understand how the powers of each Institution interrelate.

## Assessment advice

**Essay questions** in this area of European Law will commonly focus on some aspect of the relationship between two or more of the Institutions. Such questions will usually require you to have the knowledge of the functions of the Institutions, but will also require you to use that knowledge to analyse the relationships between the Institutions concerned.

**Problem questions** covering this area will generally be ones which overlap with other areas of EU law, for example relating to an aspect of an Institution's powers, like the Commission's power of enforcement under Article 226.

# Sample question

Could you answer this question? Below is a typical essay question that could arise on this topic. Guidelines on answering the question are included at the end of this chapter, whilst a sample problem question and guidance on tackling it can be found on the companion website.

'. . . it has become common to speak of an 'institutional balance' within Community institutions, and the way in which this is evoked draws on a system of checks and balances not dissimilar to those we find in more traditional governmental systems. The EU institutions have come to operate a system of checks on each other, sometimes referred to in the context of an "institutional balance" . . .'

> Douglass-Scott, S., *Constitutional Law of the European Union*,
> (Longman 2002), Chapter 2 at p.49).

To what extent does the above statement apply to the current relationship between the Commission, the Council of Ministers and the European Parliament, particularly as regards maintaining the balance of interests between the European Union and the Member States?

# ■ The Institutions of the EU

**Figure 2.1**

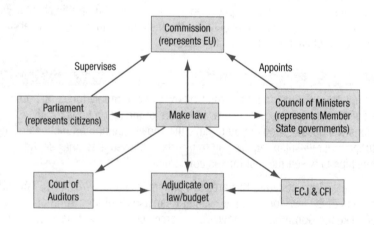

The three primary Institutions (Fig. 2.1) exist to represent different parties in the EU:

- The Council of Ministers represents the interests of the Member States' governments
- the European Parliament serves the interests of the EU citizens
- and the Commission's role is to serve the interests of the EU as an organisation.

The European Court of Justice (ECJ) and Court of First Instance (CFI) are there to adjudicate on cases arising from the Treaty, and there are additionally other Institutions which serve in an advisory or consultative role.

# Composition of the Institutions

## The European Parliament

The European Parliament is constituted of 785 MEPs directly elected by individual citizens of the EU in elections. The number of MEPs allocated to a Member State varies according to population size, with Germany as the state with the largest population size having the largest number of MEPs (99) and Malta, as the state with the smallest population, having just five. The division is criticised because it is not even – a German MEP will represent a larger number of citizens than an MEP from Luxembourg. The exact numbers after the January 2007 expansion are as follows:

| State | No. of MEPs per State |
| --- | --- |
| Germany | 99 |
| France, UK, Italy | 78 |
| Poland, Spain | 54 |
| Holland | 27 |
| Romania | 35 |
| Belgium, Czech Republic, Greece, Hungary, Portugal | 24 |
| Sweden | 19 |
| Bulgaria, Austria | 18 |
| Denmark, Finland, Slovakia | 14 |
| Ireland, Lithuania | 13 |
| Latvia | 9 |
| Slovenia | 7 |
| Cyprus, Estonia, Luxembourg | 6 |
| Malta | 5 |

Currently MEPs are only organised according to national party divisions, and are elected for a period of five years.

# The Council of the European Union (commonly the Council of Ministers)

The Council of Ministers is composed of ministerial representatives of the Member State governments. Each State will send a minister relevant to the matter being debated, and therefore the representative will vary accordingly. Each State has a number of votes, and the votes are weighted in a similar way to the weighting in the European Parliament.

| State | Number of votes in the Council of Ministers |
| --- | --- |
| Germany, France, Italy, UK | 29 |
| Spain, Poland | 27 |
| Romania | 14 |
| Holland | 13 |
| Belgium, Czech Republic, Greece, Hungary, Portugal | 12 |
| Austria, Bulgaria, Sweden | 10 |
| Denmark, Ireland, Lithuania, Slovakia, Finland | 7 |
| Estonia, Cyprus, Latvia, Luxembourg, Slovenia | 4 |
| Malta | 3 |

This makes a total of 345 votes. The Council of Ministers will vote either by Qualified Majority Voting, bare majority, or unanimity.

## KEY DEFINITION

**Qualified Majority Voting** Qualified Majority Voting (QMV) requires the following:

- A minimum of 255 out of 345 votes cast in favour
- A majority of all Member States voting in favour
- At least 62% of the EU's total population represented by the vote in favour.

# Presidency of the Council of Ministers

The Presidency is held by each of the Member States in turn, for a period of six months. During that time, the State which holds the Presidency may put forward proposals and reforms that they would like implemented, and propose policies they are in favour of. The head of government for that State represents the State as President of the Council of Ministers.

**Problem area:** The European Council

The European Council is not an official Institution of the EU, and it is important not to confuse it with the Council of Ministers. The European Council arose from unofficial meetings of the Heads of State of the Member States, and its main purpose is to discuss the policy direction of the EU.

# European Commission

The European Commission consists of one appointed Commissioner from each State. Each Commissioner will represent a different area of the Commission's business, for example trade and industry or the environment, known as a portfolio. They will also be supported by Directorates General. The President of the Commission will also choose a number of Vice-Presidents, and currently the President has five.

**EXAM TIP**

Where examination questions focus upon the Institutions, you should not use this as an opportunity to merely regurgitate facts about composition and powers of the Institutions. The study of the Institutions is as much about the intricacies of how they allow the EU to function as it is about their powers. For example, the fact that the Commission is constituted of a representative of each State goes a long way towards helping the Member States to feel involved in policy-making, and to accept policies coming out of the Commission, despite the fact that Commissioners are persons 'whose independence is beyond doubt' – Article 213.

# The European Court of Justice and Court of First Instance

The European Court of Justice (ECJ) and Court of First Instance (CFI) are each made up of one judge from each Member State, with the ECJ also having eight Advocates General, drawn from the Member States. Currently therefore, there are 27 judges in each of these two courts. Although previously, when there were fewer member States, they had been known to sit as a full chamber, the number of judges in the enlarged EU makes this difficult. They will therefore sit in groups of either three, five or a Grand Chamber of 11 – based on the nature and subject of the case itself. Although these two courts follow similar rules, there is no cross-over: e.g. a CFI judge will not sit in the ECJ.

It is important that each State has their own judge – therefore every legal tradition in the EU is represented in these two courts.

**REVISION NOTE**

Although it is important to know who the ECJ and CFI are, you will tend to find assessment questions will more readily concentrate on what they do, and how this affects the operation of the EU. For example, see Chapter 5 on the Article 234 reference procedure, or Chapters 3 and 4 on the contentious procedures that take place in the ECJ.

**Problem area:** European Court of Justice

Remember when European courts are mentioned here, that these are the EU's own courts, and they are given the role of dealing with the laws of the EU. You should not, for example, confuse the European Court of Justice (ECJ) with the European Court of Human Rights (ECHR) as this is an entirely separate court, dealing with entirely different matters, and not part of the EU structure.

# Other Institutions

There are also several other Institutions involved in the day-to-day processes of the EU:

| Institution | Role | Personnel |
| --- | --- | --- |
| Economic and Social Committee | To be consulted by the Council and Commission on legislative proposals. Can also submit their own opinion on European matters without being asked | Representatives of various groups concerned with economic activities, such as manufacturers, farmers, trade unionists, or public interest groups |
| Committee of the Regions | To be consulted by the Council and Commission on legislative proposals | Representatives of regional interests |
| Court of Auditors | To control and supervise the implementation of the budget | One member from each of the 27 Member States |

# ■ Powers of the Institutions

The powers of the primary Institutions can be broadly broken down into legislative and supervisory power, and it is a combination of these two types of power that helps with the smooth running of the EU.

## KEY DEFINITIONS

**Legislative power** The involvement of an Institution in amending, or agreeing to, legislation made by the EU under the EC Treaty.

**Supervisory power** The power of an Institution to monitor, supervise or scrutinise the actions of another Institution in the EU Institutional structure.

| Institution | Powers and duties |
|---|---|
| European Parliament (see Articles 189–201) | Participates in the legislative process. Supervises the European Commission |
| Council of the European Union (commonly referred to as the Council of Ministers) (see Articles 202–210) | Makes the final decision on legislative proposals, coordinates economic policies of the Member States, delegates power to other Institutions |
| European Commission (see Articles 211–219) | Enforcer of the Treaties. Drafts legislative proposals and initiates policy once formulated by the Council |
| European Council | Not a Treaty Institution. A political Institution that represents the Member States and drives reform in the EU |
| European Court of Justice | Hears cases directed to it under the Treaty. Hears appeals on points of law from the Court of First Instance. Rules on matters of interpretation referred to it by courts of Member States |
| Court of First Instance | Hears cases directed to it under the Treaty, including Staff Cases of the EU |

# Legislative powers

The Commission, Council of Ministers and Parliament all participate in making legislation, a process which also involves other consultative bodies including the Committee of the Regions and the Economic and Social Committee. A summary of the relationship between the Institutions when making legislation is given in Figure 2.2.

A key theme in this area is the way in which the Parliament's role in making law has increased over the past few years. Traditionally the Parliament had very few powers, because prior to 1979 the MEPs were appointed, rather than elected. Successive amendments to the legislative process have increased the involvement of the Parliament so that now, in some matters, the Parliament is placed on an equal footing with the Council of Ministers.

| Legislative procedure | Role of the European Parliament |
| --- | --- |
| Consultation procedure | Parliament has the right to be consulted |
| Cooperation procedure (Article 252)    Introduced by the Single European Act 1986 | Parliament has the right to be consulted.    Parliament has the right to object to a Council and Commission 'Common Position' but their objection can be overruled by a unanimous vote in the Council of Ministers |
| Co-decision procedure (Article 251)    Introduced by the Treaty of Maastricht 1992 | Parliament has the right to be consulted.    Parliament has the right to reject a Council and Commission 'Common Position'.    Parliament has the right to propose amendments.    The final decision on the legislative proposal is a 'co-decision' between the Parliament and the Council of Ministers |

Parliament's involvement in the legislative process has increased with successive Treaty amendments as new legislative procedures have been introduced.

# Supervisory powers

The institutions of the EU exist in a system whereby certain supervision takes place between the Institutions.

In particular, the Parliament, along with increased legislative powers, also now has the power to supervise the European Commission, and has limited supervisory powers over the Council of Ministers.

**Figure 2.2**

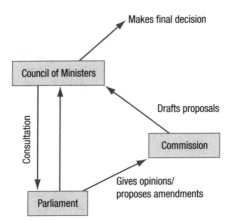

- The Parliament has the right to approve the appointment of the President of the Commission and the Commissioners (Article 214(2)), and the right of censure against the Commissioners, enabling them to dismiss the entire Commission under Article 201.
- The Commission is obliged to answer Parliament's questions, and must produce a general report which is discussed by the Parliament.
- The Council of Ministers is obliged to report three times a year to the Parliament on its recent activity.
- The President of the Council of Ministers reports to the Parliament at the beginning of the year.
- The European Parliament also runs the Committee on Petitions and appoints a European Ombudsman to investigate maladministration in any of the Institutions of the EU.

## REVISION NOTE

The European Parliament, Council of Ministers and European Commission also have the ability to challenge the activity of each other through the Article 230 and 232 procedure, as they have unlimited standing to bring an action for judicial review under this procedure. (See Chapter 4 on Judicial Review.)

The Member States also have unlimited standing under this procedure, and therefore can also scrutinise the Institutions in this way.

# Role of the European Courts

The jurisdiction of the European Courts is split between the European Court of Justice, which has existed since the signing of the European Coal and Steel Community

(ECSC) Treaty in 1952, and the Court of First Instance, which was created by the Single European Act in 1986.

The two courts share the case load of European cases – the Court of First Instance was originally created in order to assist with the growing case law of the ECJ. For example, these courts will deal with matters arising in particular areas (which are dealt with in other parts of this book) such as Judicial Review under Articles 230 and 232 (see Chapter 4), Enforcement Proceedings against Member States (Chapter 3) and will hear preliminary references from national courts under Article 234 (see Chapter 5). The two courts exist in a hierarchy, as appeals can go from the CFI to the ECJ on a point of law.

**Problem area:** Precedent

There is no system of binding precedent in the EU court system, unlike in the UK, where lower courts have to follow the rulings of higher ones. The ECJ, however, does operate a system of persuasive precedent, in that it is unlikely to depart from previous decisions in the interests of consistency but retains the freedom to do so if it feels it is appropriate.

# ■ The relationship between the Institutions

From the above information concerning how the Institutions work, we must focus upon the information about how the Institutions relate to each other (Fig. 2.3), and therefore how this can have an effect on the operation of the EU. This would also be important in approaching the essay question at the beginning of this chapter. Below are some illustrations of those relationships.

Figure 2.3

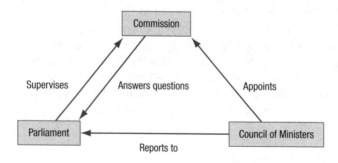

| Institutions | Relationship |
| --- | --- |
| Commission and Parliament | Parliament supervises Commission through power of censure and right to ask questions |
| Commission and Council of Ministers | Council submits policy to Commission to be legislated upon and delegates power to Commission through Comitology. Commission drafts legislation |
| Parliament and Council of Ministers | Parliament is consulted on legislative proposals. Council of Ministers reports to Parliament three times a year on activity |

## FURTHER THINKING

The relationship between the Institutions is rather complex, and certainly more complex than can be represented here. However, in order to do well in assessment questions in this area, it is important to examine the area in more detail. For example, see Lang, J. T. (2006) 'Checks and Balances in the European Union: The Institutional Structure and the "Community Method".' This article examines the system of checks and balances referred to as the 'Community Method', and argues that part of the criticism of the legal and political safeguards comes from this method being misunderstood.

# Political influences between the Institutions

The Institutions all represent different interests within the EU, and therefore when considering their exercise of powers, it is important to bear in mind who they represent. The European Commission, although appointed by the Member States, is intended to be an independent Institution, free from control of the Member State governments, and representative of the interests of the EU as a whole. The Council of Ministers represents the interests of the Member State governments, and therefore its decision making will be influenced by them, and the European Parliament is directly elected by the citizens of the EU, and will therefore take into account the interests of citizens. Bearing this in mind will therefore help with understanding the legislative and supervisory processes within the EU.

# Chapter summary:
# Putting it all together

| TEST YOURSELF |
|---|

☐ Can you tick all the points from the revision checklist at the beginning of this chapter?

☐ Take the **end-of-chapter quiz** on the companion website.

☐ Test your knowledge of the cases below with the **revision flashcards** on the website.

☐ Attempt the essay question from the beginning of the chapter using the guidelines below.

☐ Go to the companion website to try out other questions.

## Answer guidelines

### See the essay question at the start of the chapter.

This question asks about the 'Institutional balance' within the EU, and the quote refers to a system of checks and balances operating between these Institutions. This is intended to allow you to analyse the relationship between the Institutions and the way in which they are able to monitor or supervise each other.

To answer this question, you need to take into account the following:

■ The basic makeup of the three Institutions mentioned in the question, and who they represent

■ The powers of those Institutions, and how they are able to use them in a supervisory capacity, including:
  – The European Parliament's power of censure over the Commission
  – The requirement for the Council and Commission to report to the Parliament
  – The power of appointment of the Commission of the Council, and the power of approval of those appointments by the Parliament
  – The standing of the Institutions to take action under Judicial Review against any of the other Institutions

■ An analysis of how this impacts upon the operation of the EU Institutions, especially with regard to how this may influence decision making in the Institutions.

### Make your answer stand out

This question will require a certain amount of recall of information about the powers and duties of the Institutions, but in order to make your answer rise above one which merely repeats this information, you need to think about how what you know about the Institutions allows you to analyse the relationship between them. Therefore, you need to think about how the elements of supervision between the Institutions might lead to an overall 'balance' between the Institutions.

## FURTHER READING

Dashwood, A. and Johnson, A. (2004) 'The Institutions of the Enlarged EU under the Regime of the Constitutional Treaty', 41 CMLR 1481

Lang, J.T. (2006) 'Checks and Balances in the European Union: The Institutional Structure and the "Community Method"', 12 European Public Law 127–154

Peterson, J. and Bomberg, E. (1999) *Decision-Making in the European Union*. New York: Palgrave Macmillan

# 3

# Articles 226–228: Enforcement actions against Member States

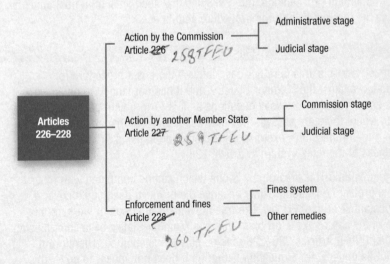

Articles 226–228

Action by the Commission
Article 226 ~~226~~ 258 TFEU
- Administrative stage
- Judicial stage

Action by another Member State
Article 227 259 TFEU
- Commission stage
- Judicial stage

Enforcement and fines
Article 228 260 TFEU
- Fines system
- Other remedies

A printable version of this topic map is available from www.pearsoned.co.uk/lawexpress

# Revision Checklist

## Essential points you should know:

☐ The purpose of enforcement actions against Member States, and their importance in ensuring the efficient functioning of the Community

☐ The substance and procedure of actions to be taken under Articles 226, 227 and 228

☐ The exercise of discretion by the Commission regarding Article 226

☐ Circumstances where Member States pursue an action under Article 227.

# Introduction:

An important part of the functioning of the EU is the enforceability of its laws. Previously in Chapter 2 we have examined the Institution's involvement in making law and in Chapter 1 we have examined its status in the legal systems of its Member States. However, at some point, whether it be deliberate or accidental, Member States run into problems of non-compatibility or conflict with EU law.

In such situations, there are mechanisms involving the European Commission and the Member States, which ensure that the conflict is resolved in the interests of the Single European Market and integration. This chapter aims to review the procedure for bringing enforcement proceedings, the principles that such an action must abide by, and discuss the reasons behind the procedure and its use.

## Assessment advice

**Essay questions** This area is rather descriptive – there is a procedure for enforcing law against the Member States – and it has not tended to be an area which is as appropriate for essay questions as it is for problem questions. However, where there are essays, they may cover areas of the procedure like, for example, the Commission's exercise of its discretion in using Article 226, or the effectiveness of the fines system in Article 228.

**Problem questions** This area of law is one which can be combined with other areas in a problem question, mainly because the problem itself could cover a more substantive area of EU law, like free movement of goods or workers, but because of the nature of the problem (if it is a Member State's behaviour causing the problem) then Articles 226–228 may be part of the solution. Therefore it would not be unusual for a question, although it does not appear to cover this area, to have elements of this area as part of its solution.

# Sample question

Could you answer this question? Below is a typical problem question that could arise on this topic. Guidelines on answering the question are included at the end of this chapter, whilst a sample essay question and guidance on tackling it can be found on the companion website.

## Problem question

The German government has recently introduced a system of import licences regarding the import of sausages into Germany. Any sausages with a fat content of more than 20% are refused a licence under their scheme. The German Agriculture Minister, Von Smallhausen, explains to the Council of Ministers that although this is regrettable, it is necessary in order to protect the wellbeing of the German people, and is part of a health policy committed to reducing the cholesterol levels of its citizens.

John Prestwick, the UK Minister of Agriculture, is incensed at this licensing scheme, and believes it is nothing more than a transparent ruse to maintain the market dominance of the German sausage producers and exclude the Great British Sausage from the German market during an economic downturn in meat products.

Prestwick writes a letter to Von Smallhausen, stating that 'unless the German government drops this idiotic licence system, I shall ask the Commission to bring the German government, Parliament and Courts before the Court of Justice for blatantly conspiring to ignore Germany's obligations towards the Free Movement of Goods principle under the EC Treaty. Failing this, the UK government will take this matter before the Court itself.'

When the UK government raises this matter with the Commission, the Commission replies that 'in the light of the current situation with the accession of new Member States into the EU and the effect of the transitional provisions involved in this, it may be better to leave this matter to next year, when the EU as a whole is more settled.'

Advise the UK government as to the possible legal remedies open to it under the EC Treaty.

# ■ Purpose of Articles 226–228

The procedure in Articles 226–228 is there to ensure that where Member States are not complying with EU law, there is an effective system of ensuring that they do comply. This has three elements to it:

■ Responsibility and powers as 'watchdog' given to a Community Institution
■ Power given to all Member States to take action where they see it is appropriate
■ System of fines to back up the system where necessary.

The way in which this system is put into practice is through a two-stage process:

■ Action taken by, or in front of, the Commission
■ Cases taken to the ECJ either by the Commission or by another Member State.

REVISION NOTE

One other way in which Member States can be liable for their failure to enact EU laws in their own systems is one discussed in Chapter 1: through the doctrine of Direct Effects. This is different from Articles 226–228 actions, because it can be pursued by individuals, and Articles 226–228 cannot. The emphasis is also different as Direct Effect is about giving effect to the law despite the actions of the Member State, and through the use of State Liability for Non-Implementation, individuals can be compensated for damage which comes directly from the State's failure. Articles 226–228 are about pursuit and punishment of the Member State, rather than compensation for individuals. They are two different ways in which action against Member States can be taken where they are not complying with Community law.

# ■ Article 226 – Action by the Commission

**KEY STATUTE**

**Article 226**

If the Commission considers that a Member State has failed to fulfil an obligation under this Treaty, it shall deliver a reasoned opinion on the matter after giving the State concerned the opportunity to submit its observations.

If the State concerned does not comply with the opinion within the period laid down by the Commission, the latter may bring the matter before the Court of Justice.

## Failure to fulfil an obligation

This is not defined in the Treaty. However, you should take a common sense approach to looking at this issue – any duty or obligation placed on a Member State that they have not complied with can fall under this definition – whether that is an obligation directly from the Treaty, or from some form of secondary legislation which has been properly enacted under the Treaty. Also, it can either be an **action** or an **omission** by the Member State. You should also bear in mind that it doesn't matter which part of the State has failed to meet an obligation: the State as a whole is responsible – see Case 77/69 *Commission* v. *Belgium* (1970) ECR 237, where the Belgian government was held to account for the failure of the Belgian Parliament to enact the relevant legislation.

## Procedure under Article 226

As mentioned above, there are two elements to this – action by the Commission, and action in the ECJ. The procedure is as follows:

**Figure 3.1**

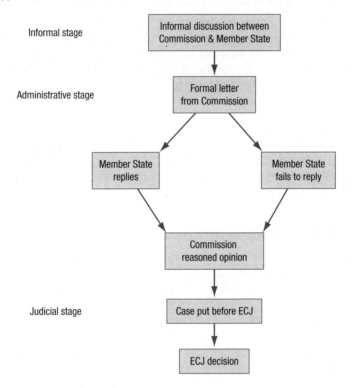

## Administrative stage

| Procedure | What it means |
| --- | --- |
| Informal letter | The Commission communicates informally and in private with a Member State about a potential breach under the Treaty. The Member State has to cooperate under its obligations in Article 10 |
| Formal notice | Formal written letter from the Commission to the Member State. Sets out what they are accused of, and asks them to respond |
| Member State response | Written response to formal notice. If the Member State fails to respond in two months, the Commission goes on to the next stage anyway |
| Commission reasoned opinion | Formal opinion from the Commission stating what the infringement is, and requiring the Member State to fix the problem. Includes a time limit for them to do so (usually two months) |

## KEY DEFINITION

**Reasoned opinion** The reasoned opinion is a written statement from the Commission, which lays down the obligation concerned, and the reasons why the Member State has failed to meet this obligation. It should clearly spell out the Commission's objection, and therefore it should be possible for the Member State to know what it needs to do to rectify this.

This procedure must be followed by the Commission, otherwise the Member State has cause to complain about their use of the procedure under Article 230 or 232. However, if this procedure is properly followed and the Member State does not comply with the Commission's reasoned opinion, then the Commission may move on to the next stage of the procedure.

### Problem area: Commission discretion

The important point to make here is the discretion that the Commission has in bringing this procedure. Article 226 says '*IF* the Commission considers that a Member State has failed to fulfil an obligation . . .' The Commission has a lot of discretion as to when it is going to take action, and for which infringements. Case 247/87 *Star Fruit Company* v. *Commission* (1989) ECR 291 shows that the Commission can't be forced to take action under Article 226.

There is also no time limit on the different actions of the Commission under the Administrative Stage, and so they can take the next step in the process when they wish, if at all. About 90% of all Article 226 actions are resolved in this stage without going to the ECJ, and the way in which the Commission manages these situations is part of this.

You should bear in mind that as a result an individual cannot force the Commission to take action, but a Member State can take action itself under Article 227. An individual is better off trying to use Direct Effects against the Member State. When revising this subject, remember there are alternatives, and that this procedure is part of a wider system. This can be an important point to remember in a problem question such as the one at the beginning of this chapter, but also in an essay question about the Commission's discretion in Article 226.

## FURTHER THINKING

Commission discretion is an important part of the flexibility of the Article 226 procedure – the Commission makes its own decisions as to which actions to pursue, but at the same time it means it can go after the more serious infringements first. For further reading on this, see Evans, A. (1979) 'The Enforcement Procedure of Article 169 EEC: Commission Discretion'. (Article 169 is the old numbering for Article 226.)

# Judicial Stage

Once the Commission has exhausted the Administrative Stage, if the Member State does not comply with its reasoned opinion within the time limit, then the Commission may take the matter to the ECJ. This is the Judicial Stage.

Points to bear in mind concerning the Judicial Stage:

■ The burden of proof lies with the Commission to prove its case
■ Even if the Member State has complied with the reasoned opinion by the time the case comes to court, the Commission may still bring the case: see Case C-240/86 *Commission* v. *Greece* (1988) ECR 1835
■ Defences put forward by the Member States are generally not accepted by the ECJ (see for example Case 128/78 *Re: Tachographs* (*Commission* v. *UK*) (1979) ECR 419 – political difficulties involving disputes with the transport unions were not an acceptable reason not to introduce new tachograph laws in the UK). The only acceptable one is that the Commission got it wrong, and that the State is not in breach of EU law.

The outcome of a case in the ECJ is as described in Article 228:

---

**KEY STATUTE**

**Article 228(1)** ✓

If the Court of Justice finds that a Member State has failed to fulfil an obligation under this Treaty, the State shall be required to take the necessary measures to comply with the judgment of the Court of Justice.

---

# ■ Article 227 – action by another Member State

Although the Commission cannot be forced to take action, another Member State has the ability to take the matter to the ECJ itself, if the Commission fails to do so. This takes place under Article 227.

---

**KEY STATUTE**

**Article 227(1)**

A Member State which considers that another Member State has failed to fulfil an obligation under this Treaty may bring the matter before the Court of Justice.

---

# Procedure under Article 227

The procedure (Fig. 3.2) followed here is very similar to that of Article 226. Article 227(2) states that the matter has to be brought before the Commission by the two Member States concerned before it can go to the ECJ, so the Commission still has an involvement here.

**Figure 3.2**

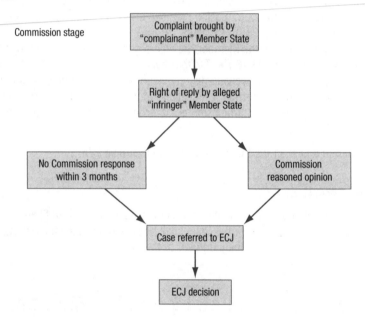

Commission stage

Complaint brought by "complainant" Member State

Right of reply by alleged "infringer" Member State

No Commission response within 3 months

Commission reasoned opinion

Case referred to ECJ

ECJ decision

## EXAM TIP

Although the Commission is still involved in Article 227, the thing to remember is that they are not able to delay or dictate the timing of the action taken here. This may be important if the Commission refused to take action themselves under Article 226. It is also important to remember this if you are being asked to advise a Member State in a problem question.

There is a time limit of three months, and if within that time the Commission has not issued a reasoned opinion, then the Member State is able to take its case to the ECJ without a reasoned opinion.

## Problems with Article 227

Article 227 actions that go all the way to the ECJ are rare. This is mainly because it is much more straightforward to get the Commission to pursue the action under Article 226, and also they can cause problems between the two States at dispute with each other (there can be damage to diplomatic relations). There have only been three cases to date that resulted in a judgment from the ECJ, Case 141/78 *France* v. *UK* (1979) ECR 2923, Case C-388/95 *Belgium* v. *Spain* (2000) ECR I-3123 and Case C-145/04 *Spain* v. *UK* (2006) ECR I-7917.

# ■ Article 228 – enforcement and fines

Usually, a successful action under Article 226 or 227 will result in the Member State complying with their obligations under the Treaty. In a few very unusual situations, it may be necessary to use the enforcement section of Article 228. This requires two steps to be taken:

■ Another reasoned opinion from the Commission has to be issued to the offending Member State
■ A second action in the ECJ in order to decide on the fine amount to be imposed upon the Member State.

Factors that are taken into account when deciding the amount to fine are:

■ The seriousness of the breach and the length of time that has passed since that breach
■ The financial size (by Gross Domestic Product) of the Member State
■ Whether to impose a lump sum fine, or one which increases daily.

### FURTHER THINKING

Article 228's fines system was only recently introduced in order to give more teeth to enforcement of Community law against the Member States – without it, a State could ignore political pressure from the Community and continue to act in infringement of their obligations. This system aims to avoid cases lingering for many years. See Wenneras, P. (2006) 'A New Dawn for Commission Enforcement under Articles 226 and 228 EC: General and Persistent (GAP) Infringements, Lump Sums and Penalty Payments'.

## Other remedies available in Articles 226–228 actions

Articles 226–228 actions can be very lengthy. Some cases can drag on for years, the most extreme example being the *Commission* v. *France* case [2006] ECR-I 2461 which lasted from 1973 to 1994! It may be necessary to make interim orders – those that provide a temporary solution to the problem while the case is still being decided:

| Treaty Article | Description |
|---|---|
| Article 242 | Interim injunction from ECJ to suspend a piece of legislation from a Member State that is breaching Community Law |
| Article 243 | Interim measures which can be put in place by the ECJ where there is damage to an individual's interests or economic hardship |

# Chapter summary:
# Putting it all together

☐ Can you tick all the points from the revision checklist at the beginning of this chapter?

☐ Take the **end-of-chapter quiz** on the companion website.

☐ Test your knowledge of the cases below with the **revision flashcards** on the website.

☐ Attempt the problem question from the beginning of the chapter using the guidelines below.

☐ Go to the companion website to try out other questions.

## Answer guidelines

**See the problem question at the start of the chapter.**

This question requires a knowledge of two areas, Articles 226–228 as covered in this chapter, but also free movement of goods as shown in Chapter 6. The basic points on free movement of goods will be mentioned here, but you will need to look at the relevant law in that chapter. Remember that this question is asking you to analyse the situation from the point of view of the UK government.

You will need to bear in mind the following issues in your answer:

■ The most likely breach to Germany's obligations is through the free movement of goods provisions in Article 28

■ The licensing restrictions are likely to be seen as a MEQR (Measure having an Equivalent Effect to a Quantitative Restriction)

■ The claims on protecting the health of the German people are likely to be dismissed following the *Cassis de Dijon* case

■ So, you need to look at Article 226, whether it can be used here, and whether the Commission can be forced to act here – look at the Commission's discretion section (above)

■ What procedure would need to be followed? Break it down into administrative and judicial procedure and explain what is needed in each one

■ If the Commission is unwilling to follow the Article 226 procedure, look at Article 227 as an alternative – what rights do the UK government have to bring the action? Examine the extent to which they can follow this procedure without the influence of the Commission.

■ Finally, Article 228(2) should be used if the German government still refuses to cooperate, as this can impose a fine upon them for non-compliance.

## Make your answer stand out

As this is an area heavily dominated by procedure, it is easy to just list the procedure as your answer. Take some time to think about the policy behind the procedure. The Commission's discretion allows flexibility in the application of Article 226, for example. Similarly Article 227 is used rarely because of the potential for political problems. Examiners like students to have analysed a situation and to be able to produce answers which demonstrate a good understanding of the area, rather than ones that show they have just memorised a lot of facts and reproduced them.

## FURTHER READING

Evans, A. (1979) 'The Enforcement Procedure of Article 169 EEC: Commission Discretion', 4 European Law Review 442

Wenneras, P. (2006) 'A New Dawn for Commission Enforcement under Articles 226 and 228 EC: General and Persistent (GAP) Infringements, Lump Sums and Penalty Payments', 43 CML Rev 31

# 4

# Articles 230 and 232: Judicial Review

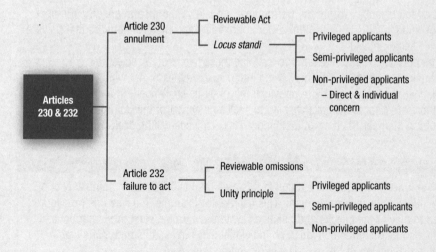

A printable version of this topic map is available from www.pearsoned.co.uk/lawexpress

# Revision Checklist

## Essential points you should know:

- [ ] The underlying purpose for Judicial Review actions in the ECJ
- [ ] The Community Acts that can be annulled and the grounds for that annulment
- [ ] The Institutions that can be compelled to act in the absence of action, and the grounds for this
- [ ] The *locus standi* of an applicant for an action under Article 230 or 232
- [ ] The unity principle binding Articles 230 and 232 together.

# Introduction:

The ability to challenge a binding Act of the Community through Judicial Review is an important part of the Community's legal system. Articles 230 and 232 contain the main procedures for Judicial Review of Community law. These procedures have two purposes, to either annul an improperly enacted law, or to compel an Institution of the EU to act in a situation where it has not done so, in contravention of its duties under the Treaties.

This procedure is important because of the way that it fits in with the system of checks and balances within the Community – it allows the Institutions, the Member States and individuals to scrutinise Community law and therefore ensure that powers are not being abused.

The purpose of this chapter is to examine these two treaty Articles, the circumstances in which they may come into play, the types of Act which may be challenged, and the grounds upon which they may be challenged. In particular, the rules are more strict for individuals wishing to challenge an Act of the Community, rather than for a Member State or an Institution. This last issue will be dealt with separately.

## Assessment advice

**Essay questions** Essay questions in this area tend to focus upon some aspect of the Judicial Review mechanism. This can be, for example, the role this procedure has to play in the checks and balances system set up between the Institutions; it can also be the difficulty which an individual faces in establishing *locus standi* and a discussion of the case law surrounding this issue.

**Problem questions** Problem questions on the other hand are more unusual, as they have to involve the creation of a scenario. This therefore can tend to focus upon the *locus standi* issue, as this will involve individuals.

# Sample question

Could you answer this question? Below is a typical essay question that could arise on this topic. Guidelines on answering the question are included at the end of this chapter, whilst a sample problem question and guidance on tackling it can be found on the companion website.

| Essay question |
| --- |

Community Law 'positively discriminates' against any natural or legal person who might wish to pursue an action under Articles 230 and 232 (ex Articles 173 and 175).

**Discuss.**

# ■ Article 230 – annulment of a Community Act

**KEY STATUTE**

### Article 230(1) EC

The Court of Justice shall review the legality of Acts adopted jointly by the European Parliament and the Council, of Acts of the Council, of the Commission and of the ECB, other than recommendations and opinions, and of Acts of the European Parliament intended to produce legal effects vis-à-vis third parties.

Article 230 is the Community's judicial review procedure (Fig. 4.1) – allowing the European Court of Justice to review binding Acts of the Community. The purpose is to ensure accountability of the Institutions for action taken by them, and to allow different parties to challenge them.

# ■ Reviewable Acts

Article 230 states that any Act of the Community, other than recommendations and opinions, can be reviewed. The key distinction here lies with the binding nature of the Act – recommendations and opinions are not reviewable because they are not binding. However, any other Act of the Community (see Article 249 and Chapter 2 on Sources of Law) can be challenged.

**Figure 4.1**

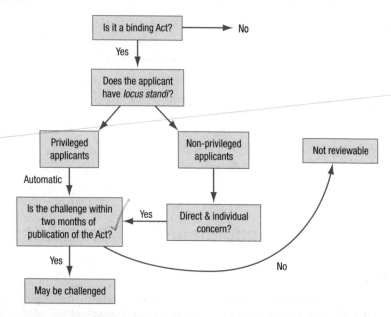

**REVISION NOTE**

Only secondary sources of law are dealt with by this area of the Treaty – Treaty Articles themselves cannot be challenged. See Chapter 2 for a fuller examination of those sources of law. In this chapter, where it refers to a 'Community Act', then it concerns these secondary sources of law.

# *Locus standi*: the ability to challenge an Act

Probably the most important aspect of Article 230 (and 232) is the ability to challenge an Act. If you do not have *locus standi*, then you cannot take action here. Lack of *locus standi* will result in a case being thrown out immediately.

For the purposes of Articles 230 and 232, those eligible to challenge a Community Act are split into three categories:

| Category | Members of this category |
| --- | --- |
| Privileged Applicants | Commission, Council of Ministers, European Parliament, all Member States |
| Semi-privileged applicants | European Central Bank, Court of Auditors |
| Non-privileged applicants | Private Individuals (including companies) |

# Privileged applicants

**KEY STATUTE**

### Article 230(2)

It shall for this purpose have jurisdiction in actions brought by a Member State, the European Parliament, the Council or the Commission on grounds of lack of competence, infringement of an essential procedural requirement, infringement of this Treaty or of any rule of law relating to its application, or misuse of powers.

Those in this category are deemed to have a general interest in Community Acts, and therefore can challenge any reviewable Act. The fact that these parties will all have taken part in some way in passing this legislation in the first place does not disqualify them. This point was made in Case 166/78 *Italy* v. *EC Council* (1979) ECR 2575. The European Parliament has only recently been added to this category, as part of the increase in its influence and power within the Community.

**EXAM TIP**

The exercise of Articles 230 and 232 is an important part of the system of 'checks and balances' within the Community. In particular, because the European Parliament now has Privileged Applicant status, it adds to its supervisory powers. Any answer to an essay question concerning the supervisory powers of the European Parliament (see Chapter 2 on the Institutions) should make this point.

# Semi-privileged applicants

**KEY STATUTE**

### Article 230(3)

The Court of Justice shall have jurisdiction under the same conditions in actions brought by the Court of Auditors and by the ECB for the purpose of protecting their prerogatives.

The Court of Auditors and the European Central Bank can challenge a Community Act if the law in question affects or changes one of their powers.

# Non-privileged applicants

> **KEY STATUTE**
>
> ## Article 230(4)
>
> Any natural or legal person may, under the same conditions, institute proceedings against a decision addressed to that person or against a decision which, although in the form of a regulation or a decision addressed to another person, is of direct and individual concern to the former.

Private persons and companies are classed as 'non-privileged' because they have to prove that they should be entitled to challenge a Community Act. This is the most controversial area of this subject, because it very heavily restricts a non-privileged applicant's ability to challenge an Act. Article 230(4) allows an individual to challenge where:

- it concerns a **decision** which is addressed to the person; or
- it concerns a **decision** or a **regulation** equivalent to a decision that is of direct and individual concern to that person.

This restricts the type of Community Act which can be challenged, and the circumstances in which it can be challenged, leaving a very narrow window indeed.

The first of these two categories will be fairly easy to deal with – decisions addressed to individuals are self-evident. A directive or regulation of direct and individual concern must fulfil three criteria: it must be equivalent to a decision, and of direct and individual concern to the person.

## It must be equivalent to a decision

A regulation is described in Article 249(2) as having general application, but regulations that have been aimed at individuals or groups have been held to be equivalent to a decision in the way they behave. For example, this was the case in Case 41–44/70 *International Fruit Co.* v. *Commission* (1971) ECR 411. If a regulation does have general application, then it cannot be challenged by an individual.

## FURTHER THINKING: RELAXATION OF THE RULES IN *CODORNIU* v. *COUNCIL*

Case C-309/89 *Codorniu* v. *EC Council* (1994) ECR I-1853 relaxed the rules on whether regulations with general application could be challenged by individuals. Although normally any Act of general application cannot be challenged by individuals, in *Codorniu* the regulation did have general application, but could still be challenged because it had particular concern to Codorniu. This was a bold move because the ECJ were saying that it had both general and specific applications at the same time. Unfortunately this has not had the effect of generally relaxing the rules, as it hasn't subsequently been followed.

See Arnull, A. (2001) 'Private Applicants and the Action for Annulment since Codorniu'.

# It must be of direct and individual concern to the person

Individual concern

**KEY CASE**

### Case 25/62 *Plaumann* v. *Commission* (1963) ECR 95

### Concerning: the test for individual concern

### Facts

This was a decision aimed at the German government instructing them to lift an import duty on clementines going into Germany. Plaumann claimed direct and individual concern.

### Legal principle

They would be individually concerned if the decision affected them 'by reason of certain attributes which are peculiar to them or by reason of circumstances in which they are differentiated from all other persons'.

Some examples of the application of this are set out in the Table below.

| Individual concern | Case |
| --- | --- |
| As part of a class of political parties affected by the decision | Case 294/83 '*Les Verts*' v. *Parliament* (1986) ECR 1339 |
| If the applicant has been involved in the legislative process used to make the law | Case T-585/93 *Stichtig Greenpeace* v. *Commission* (1995) ECR II-2205 |
| If the applicant is a trade association representing the interests of those who are individually concerned | Case T-447–449/93 *AITEC* v. *Commission* (1995) ECR II-1971 |

**Problem area:** Fixed, closed class

The case law in this area has defined the concept of a fixed, closed class rather strictly. Following on from the test (above) in *Plaumann*, there have been several cases that denied *locus standi* to applicants on this basis. This is an important issue in answering questions on individual concern. For example, following the *Plaumann* criteria, in Case T-47/95 *Terres Rouges Consultant* v. *EC Commission*, the court did not grant standing to a company that had a 70% monopoly in importing bananas – because the class they were in could be joined by anyone else. The key here is: are you in a class that makes you different from everyone else, a class that cannot be joined by anyone else? If so, then you are in a fixed, closed class.

## Direct concern

Direct concern merely means that the Community Act is directly applicable to the individual, without any need for the Member States to enact any further laws or have any further discretion.

For example, Case 10 & 18/68 *Eridana* v. *Commission* (1969) ECR 459, where although this concerned granting of aid by the Commission, the decision as to who was given the aid was made by the Italian government.

### EXAM TIP

The consequence of such strict requirements for non-privileged applicants is that very few actions may be brought by private individuals. This may seem to be rather harsh; however, when discussing this area, it is worth bearing in mind that there are also important policy reasons for doing this: if the *locus standi* test were broader, then the consequence would likely be the clogging of the European courts with actions brought by those who aren't immediately affected by them. You should bear this in mind, especially if your exam asks you to discuss the position of private parties under this action.

# Time limit

Article 230(5) sets a time limit of two months from date of publication, or from the date the applicant knew about the Act.

# Reasons to challenge a Community Act

| Reason | Example |
|---|---|
| Lack of competence | Each Institution must only act within the powers given to it by the Treaty.<br>    See Case C-327/91 *France* v. *Commission* (1994) ECR I-3641 where the Commission signed an international agreement that should have been done by the Council |
| Infringement of an essential procedural requirement | Failing to follow proper procedure.<br>    See Case 139/79 *Maizena* v. *Council* (1980) ECR 3393 where the Council failed to consult the European Parliament, where they were obliged to under the Treaty |
| Infringement of the Treaty | A very broad term, which could include all general principles of EU law.<br>    Case 101/76 *KSH* v. *Intervention Board* (1977) ECR 797 involved the general principle of the right to be heard |
| Misuse of powers | Where an Institution uses its powers for the wrong purpose |

# ■ Article 232 – action for failure to act

Actions under Articles 230 and 232 are very closely linked under the **unity principle**, therefore the rules concerning how Articles 230 and 232 are used run parallel. They can also be pleaded at the same time, because a failure to act can also be seen as an Institution acting improperly.

## *Locus standi*

The rules concerning *locus standi* are similar, but more restrictive than those for Article 230.

| Article | Applicants |
|---|---|
| Article 232(1) – privileged applicants | Institutions as discussed in Article 230(2) |
| Article 232(3) – non-privileged applicants | Private individuals as discussed in Article 230(4) |

**Problem area:** Non-privileged applicants in Article 232

The main problem here is that Article 232 is even more restrictive than Article 230, **because it doesn't even allow applicants who have 'direct and individual concern'** as Article 230 does. The only individuals who can use Article 232 are those to whom a decision **should** have been addressed.

**KEY CASE**

**Case 246/81 *Lord Bethel* v. *Commission* (1982) ECR 2277**

**Concerning:** *locus standi* for an individual challenging a failure to act

**Facts**

Lord Bethel challenged the Commission's failure to take action against airline price fixing. The Commission claimed he did not have *locus standi*.

**Legal principle**

The ECJ decided that as any decision from the Commission concerning the price fixing would not be addressed to him, then he did not have standing to challenge the Commission's failure to act.

# Reviewable omissions

Article 232 is about duties under the Treaty. So if an Institution has failed to act, and the Treaty states that they should have, then this may be a reviewable omission. It must be a clear duty under the Treaty, and so if this is not the case, then there is no action. For example, in Case 13/83 *European Parliament* v. *Commission* (1985) ECR 1513, the obligation placed on the Commission by the Treaty, was not worded precisely enough for a failure to perform this obligation to be a failure to act under the meaning of Article 232.

# Article 232 procedure

**Problem area:** Institution defines its position

Where an Institution defines its position, this can be an easy way for it to avoid action under Article 232. The Treaty doesn't define what this is, but if an Institution justifies why it has not acted, then it may escape the action being brought under Article 232. The ECJ has held actions inadmissible where this was the case. The procedure under Article 232 is illustrated in Figure 4.2.

**Figure 4.2**

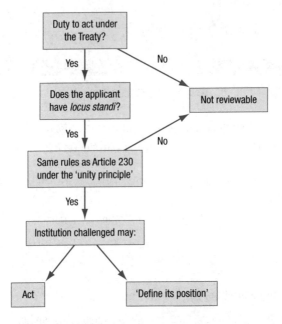

EXAM TIP

Because the two areas of Articles 230 and 232 are so closely linked under the **unity principle**, it is worth bearing this in mind when preparing for exams – as long as you are able to identify the few differences between the two actions, then you can consider the two actions together – action taken in the ECJ can tend to include both an Article 230 and an Article 232 action at the same time.

# ■ The consequences: Articles 230 and 232

Where an action is successful in either Article 230 or 232, the consequence is the same: Article 233 states that the Institution must 'comply with the judgment of the Court of Justice'.

# Chapter summary:
# Putting it all together

## TEST YOURSELF

☐ Can you tick all the points from the revision checklist at the beginning of this chapter?

☐ Take the **end-of-chapter quiz** on the companion website.

☐ Test your knowledge of the cases below with the **revision flashcards** on the website.

☐ Attempt the essay question from the beginning of the chapter using the guidelines below.

☐ Go to the companion website to try out other questions.

## Answer guidelines

**See the essay question at the start of the chapter.**

Consider what this question is asking you. As we have discussed in this chapter, the requirements for private persons who wish to take action under Articles 230 and 232 are much more restrictive than for the Institutions and Member States. This question is asking you to consider two issues:

▌ First, the way in which private persons are restricted, through the two requirements in the Treaty that the measure is either addressed to that person, or of direct and individual concern to them. In particular, direct and individual concern has been narrowly interpreted through the use of the phrase 'fixed, closed class'. Look at the key cases such as *Plaumann* and *International Fruit*, and how they have interpreted the meaning of this. Comment on the effect this has had on a private individual's right to bring an action.

▌ Secondly, consider why the ECJ has been this restrictive in interpreting the Treaty. The *Codorniu* case shows some of the policy arguments behind how it has interpreted the idea of class. Think about the potential problems of overloading the courts with actions, for example.

**Make your answer stand out**

This is an area of law that is heavily based upon the cases. There are many cases which provide good examples of the operation of this rule, for example where they are part of a fixed, closed class (such as Case C-152/88 *Sofrimport*), or where they have taken part in making the legislation (such as Case T-585/93 *Stichtig Greenpeace*), or restrictions on trade associations (such as Case T-447–449/93 *AITEC*). You can make your answer stand out by your use of cases which show the ECJ's development of the law in this area, going beyond merely looking at the most significant cases here.

## FURTHER READING

Albors-Llorens, A. (2003) 'The Standing of Private Parties to Challenge Community Measures: Has the European Court Missed the Boat?', 62 Cambridge Law Journal 72

Arnull, A. (2001) 'Private Applicants and the Action for Annulment since *Codorniu'*, 38 CMLR 7

Cooke, J. (1997) '*Locus Standi* of Private Parties Under Article 173(4)', 6 IJEL 4

Craig, P. (1994) 'Legality, Standing and Substantive Review in Community Law', 14 Oxford Journal of Legal Studies 507

# 5

# Article 234: Preliminary rulings in the ECJ

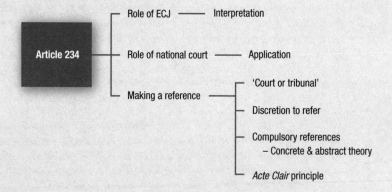

Article 234

- Role of ECJ ——— Interpretation
- Role of national court ——— Application
- Making a reference
  - 'Court or tribunal'
  - Discretion to refer
  - Compulsory references
    – Concrete & abstract theory
  - *Acte Clair* principle

A printable version of this topic map is available from www.pearsoned.co.uk/lawexpress

# Revision Checklist

## Essential points you should know:

- [ ] The purpose behind the Article 234 reference procedure and its use
- [ ] Who may make a reference to the ECJ for interpretation
- [ ] The powers of a national court in making a reference and what must be done with it once received back from the ECJ
- [ ] Obligations of a national court in circumstances where a reference is compulsory
- [ ] The ECJ's powers in dealing with a matter referred to them by a national court.

# Introduction:

Article 234 deals with references made to the European Court of Justice (ECJ) on matters of interpretation of European Community law. (Please refer to Chapter 2 for an explanation of the ECJ.) This part of the ECJ's jurisdiction differs from other aspects of its work primarily because Article 234 references are not cases that the ECJ is dealing with directly, but instead are those dealt with by a national court, which will refer questions to the ECJ.

Article 234 is important because of the consistency of interpretation that it provides. The procedure is a cooperative one, between the ECJ and the national courts of Member States. In this procedure, the ECJ provides the interpretation, and the national court is then given the responsibility to apply that interpretation to the case (Fig. 5.1). This ensures that a consistent approach to interpretation of European Community law is maintained, and it creates a clear link between national law and Community law.

In assessments, you must always bear in mind the division of roles in this procedure – each court has an important role to play, and neither court is considered to be in a superior position to the other – there is no hierarchy here, unlike in traditional relationships between courts. Therefore questions can arise which focus upon the relationship between the national court and ECJ in this procedure, or on the respective roles that each court has.

**Figure 5.1**

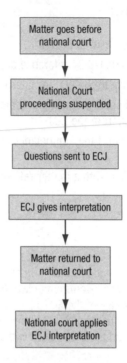

---
**Assessment advice**
---

When Article 234 is the sole area examined in an examination question, it will commonly be dealt with as an essay, although it may also form part of a question which touches on other areas as well.

**Essay questions** Both essay and problem questions can focus upon the relationship between the national court and ECJ generally, or can concentrate upon one aspect of the procedure. For example, the development of the principles surrounding the issue of what a court of last instance constitutes, or discussion of the CILFIT principle (see Case 283/81 *CILFIT* v. *Ministro della Sanità* (1982) ECR 3415) which gives us criteria where a national court may decline the opportunity to make a reference to the ECJ, are both examples which have been used in the past. The CILFIT principle and the case it is from are explained later in this chapter.

**Problem questions** Article 234's relevance to wider topics can often appear in problem questions concerning cases before national courts – there can be a case for making a reference to the ECJ as part of the issues raised by the problem.

## Sample question

Could you answer this question? Below is a typical essay question that could arise on this topic. Guidelines on answering the question are included at the end of this chapter, whilst a sample problem question and guidance on tackling it can be found on the companion website.

Essay question

The decision of the High Court in *Arsenal Football Club* v. *Reed* [2001] 2 CMLR 23 illustrates very well that the procedure set out in Article 234 is not an appeals procedure. It was intended to ensure the full collaboration of the municipal courts and the European Court of Justice. This was in order to better develop and enforce EU law in an atmosphere of mutual regard for their relative jurisdictions.

Examine the extent to which this statement correctly states the purpose underlying Article 234.

# ■ The Article 234 procedure

**KEY STATUTE**

### Article 234

The Court of Justice shall have jurisdiction to give preliminary rulings concerning:

■ the interpretation of this Treaty;
■ the validity and interpretation of Acts of the institutions of the Community and of the ECB;
■ the interpretation of the statutes of bodies established by an Act of the Council, where those statutes so provide.

Where such a question is raised before any court or tribunal of a Member State, that court or tribunal may, if it considers that a decision on the question is necessary to enable it to give judgment, request the Court of Justice to give a ruling thereon.

Where any such question is raised in a case pending before a court or tribunal of a Member State against whose decisions there is no judicial remedy under national law, that court or tribunal shall bring the matter before the Court of Justice.

**Problem area:** Treaty article renumbering

Article 234 was referred to as Article 177 under the previous numbering of the Treaty. Cases prior to the renumbering refer to the old number, and it is therefore important to bear this in mind when reading the judgments of these cases.

# Role of the European Court of Justice

The principle underlying the Article 234 procedure is cooperation. The ECJ has an important role to play in this, providing a consistent interpretation of matters of European law which is then uniformly applied throughout the EU. The ECJ can answer questions on:

- interpretation of the EC Treaty
- validity/interpretation of Acts of the Institutions
- interpretation of international agreements between the EU and third party states
- interpretation of other international agreements, for example those of the World Trade Organization
- whether a Community Act produces direct effects.

It is important to emphasise that the jurisdiction of the ECJ extends no further than the answering of questions put to it by national courts – it cannot proactively deal with matters itself under a strict policy of non-interference. Once it has answered questions put to it, it cannot involve itself with the application of those answers; see *Arsenal Football Club* v. *Reed* [2001] 2 CMLR 23 below.

# Powers of the European Court of Justice to answer questions

The ECJ has powers to deal with any questions of interpretation that are laid before it by a national court under this procedure. It does not choose the questions, and it cannot influence national courts in their choice of questions. It does, however, have the power to decide that questions are invalid. It can do so on various grounds. Below are some examples:

| Requirement of a question | Example |
| --- | --- |
| The question must be necessary for the national court to be able to give judgment | See Case 13/68 *Salgoil SA* v. *Italian Minister of Foreign Trade* (1968) ECR 453 |
| The question must not be a hypothetical one | See Case 244/80 Foglia v Novello (No.2) (1981) ECR 3045, where the ECJ refused a reference on the grounds that the proceedings had created an artificial situation in order to have a question answered |
| The ECJ may select which questions to answer | See Case 6/64 *Costa* v. *ENEL* [1964] ECR 585 |
| The ECJ may not rewrite questions | |
| The referring case must still be active | In order for the ruling to be meaningful, the case must not have been decided before the matter reaches the ECJ – therefore cases are suspended while a reference is made |

# The boundary between the power of the ECJ and the power of the national court

The use of Article 234 is intended to be cooperative in nature, and therefore it is clear that the ECJ interprets, and the national court applies. However, there have been areas where overlap has occurred, causing friction.

KEY CASE

### *Arsenal Football Club* v. *Reed* [2001] 2 CMLR 23

**Concerning: reference to ECJ; interpretation of EC law; duty of national court to follow ECJ ruling**

Facts

The *Arsenal* case concerned a reference made to the ECJ asking several questions on the interpretation of the First Trade Marks Directive 89/104/EC. The case concerned Arsenal suing a seller of unofficial Arsenal merchandise (scarves, replica shirts, etc) in defence of its registered trademark in the Arsenal logo that appears on all its merchandise. The referral was made because the UK law on trade marks was based on the Trade Marks Directive.

Legal principle

In answering the questions laid down by the High Court, the ECJ also made comments that Laddie J considered to be applying the principles to the facts, which he considered to be outside the powers of the ECJ under Article 234. He therefore applied what he saw as the interpretation, and disregarded anything he considered to be application to the facts. Although his decision was subsequently overturned by the Court of Appeal, the principle still, in theory, stands – it is not the place of the ECJ to decide the case, but to provide the interpretation to allow the national court to do this.

## FURTHER THINKING

Because the *Arsenal* case was overruled by the Court of Appeal, the principle (above) isn't given very much gravity – however, the principle is an important one, and goes to the heart of the Article 234 procedure. The ECJ must not overstep its role in this procedure to the detriment of the national court's sovereignty.

See: Saunders, O. (2004) 'A warning shot across the bows of the ECJ: The lessons of *Arsenal Football Club* v. *Reed*'.

# ■ Who may make a reference to the ECJ?

Article 234 refers to 'any court or tribunal'. This is not clearly defined, but subsequent cases have provided details as to what this means. Obviously the courts in the main judicial system would fall within this definition, but there are also many other tribunals that may wish to refer issues to the ECJ.

## KEY DEFINITION

**Court or tribunal** This is a matter of Community law – it does not matter whether the Member State recognises the body as a court, if the EU recognises it as such. It should have a judicial function, and have independence from the parties concerned.

The key elements of what the EU considers to be a court or tribunal are:

- Independence from the parties
- Performance of a judicial function
- Permanence.

You should bear in mind that the Member State may not consider it to be a court or tribunal, but that does not matter, as long as the ECJ considers it to be one.

---

**KEY CASE**

**Case 246/80** *Broekmeulen* v. *Huisarts Registratie Commissie* **[1981] ECR 2311**

**Concerning: definition of 'court or tribunal'**

**Facts**

This case concerned the Dutch medical association responsible for registering doctors in the Netherlands. The committee was the appeals committee for the Society, usually regarding the registration of a doctor to practise in the Netherlands. It dealt with cases which had already been through another judicial committee of the Society. Although this was a private body, registration was important because it was not possible to practise medicine in that country without this registration. Broekmeulen had appealed to this committee when his registration to practise was refused. In dealing with his case, a reference to the ECJ was made, and the issue as to whether the appeals committee was a 'court or tribunal' for the purposes of European law.

**Legal principle**

The ECJ decided that the appeals committee was a court or tribunal, despite the fact that Dutch law did not recognise it as such, because, as the ECJ said, it 'operates with the consent of the public authorities and their cooperation, and ... after an adversarial procedure, delivers decisions which are recognised as final'. It therefore had all the necessary qualities that the court thought necessary for a body to be considered a court or tribunal for the purposes of EU law.

---

# Exclusions

There are a couple of specific exclusions, domestic tribunals and arbitrators.

## Domestic tribunals

For example, the element that was missing from Case 138/80 *Re Jules Borker* [1980] ECR 1975 was its recognition by the public authorities. This case concerned a committee of the Paris Bar Association, and in refusing the reference, the ECJ decided that it was 'not handling a lawsuit which it has the statutory function to decide'.

## Arbitrators

Arbitrators are often not recognised as a 'court or tribunal' because parties have usually volunteered to refer their case to arbitration rather than being compelled to do so. For example, Case 102/81 *Nordsee Hochseefischerei GmbH* [1982] ECR 1095 was one where the procedure was adversarial in nature, just like the *Broekmeulen* case above. However, because the parties had previously agreed that in the event of a dispute they would go to the arbitrator (rather than the courts), then the ECJ decided that it was not a 'court or tribunal'. This was a private agreement, so the 'public' element was missing, therefore it wasn't a court.

---

### EXAM TIP

Although it may seem to be an obvious definition when answering a problem question, it is important to be able to establish definitively that a particular court or tribunal falls within the definition under Article 234, especially as this differs from national ideas of 'court or tribunal'. Don't assume that the examiner will consider this issue obvious.

---

# ■ National court discretion to refer

When questions are raised in national courts which concern EU law, the national court has a choice whether to refer to the ECJ. The Treaty puts it as follows:

### KEY STATUTE

**Article 234(2)**

Where such a question is raised before any court or tribunal of a Member State, that court or tribunal may, if it considers that a decision on the question is necessary to enable it to give judgment, request the Court of Justice to give a ruling thereon.

The decision to refer a matter to the ECJ for interpretation lies with the national court. It cannot be compelled to make a reference, either by the parties concerned or the ECJ themselves, in a situation where Article 234(2) applies.

However, any reference made by a national court must be one genuinely needed for the case in hand. For example:

---

**KEY CASE**

*Commissioners of Customs & Excise* v. *Samex ApS* (1983) 3 CMLR 194

**Concerning: appropriateness of reference to ECJ; questions to raise**

### Facts

This case concerned the High Court's attempts to deal with European Regulations concerning an import licence that one of the parties, an acrylic yarn importer, was attempting to secure. In its deliberations, the court discussed the appropriateness of a reference to the ECJ, and what questions would be in order.

### Legal principle

Bingham J pointed out in this case that where a party was attempting to use an Article 234 reference as a delaying tactic, this would justify the court's refusal to make a reference to the ECJ. This could otherwise be a delaying tactic, based upon the lengthy time it takes a reference to go through the Article 234 process. The other party would meanwhile be denied a remedy in the matter.

---

# National court compulsory references

There are some circumstances where a national court **has** to refer questions to the ECJ. As stated in the Treaty:

---

**KEY STATUTE**

**Article 234(3)**

Where any such question is raised in a case pending before a court or tribunal of a Member State against whose decisions there is no judicial remedy under national law, that court or tribunal shall bring the matter before the Court of Justice.

---

In other words:

- If there is no right of appeal; and
- there are questions of EU law that need to be answered; then
- the national court **must** make a reference to the ECJ.

| KEY DEFINITION |
| --- |

**Making a reference** A national court makes a reference to the ECJ by putting together a list of questions for interpretation and submitting them for the ECJ to consider and provide interpretation.

Article 234(3) places an obligation on certain courts to make a reference to the ECJ in certain circumstances. Where a question is raised in a court where it is not possible to appeal, then that question must be referred under the Article 234 procedure. Such a court is referred to as a 'court of last instance'.

| KEY DEFINITION |
| --- |

**Court of last instance** A court of last instance is the last court in a particular court structure that cases can go to. Therefore this means that once the case has been heard by this court, there is no route of appeal to another court. The House of Lords, as the highest court in England and Wales, is the best example of this in the UK court system.

There have been two approaches to this issue:

| Concrete theory | Abstract theory |
| --- | --- |
| The court of last instance is one from which there is no appeal in this **case**. | The court of last instance is only the one from which there is no appeal from this **court.** |

**Problem area:** Concrete vs abstract theory

It is important to clearly understand the difference here. The abstract theory was initially favoured by the UK judiciary – see Lord Denning's judgment in *Bulmer* v. *Bollinger* (1974) Ch 401, because this meant only the House of Lords fell under an *obligation* to refer questions to the ECJ – however, the ECJ favoured the concrete theory, as shown in Case 6/64 *Costa* v. *ENEL*, whereby if the case at hand cannot be appealed to a higher court, then Article 234(3) applies. Agreement with this approach from judges in the UK can be seen in *Hagen* v. *Fratelli* (1980) 3 CMLR 253 at 255.

**EXAM TIP**

The issues surrounding the concrete vs the abstract theories have now been settled, and the UK judges have fallen into line with the thinking of the ECJ, in using the concrete theory (concerning appeal in this **case**). However, as the development of this procedure can be important in any discussion in an essay question, it is still vital for you to understand this, particularly as Article 234 is still split into mandatory and discretionary references.

# The exception to Article 234(3): the *CILFIT* principle

**KEY CASE**

**Case 283/81 *CILFIT and Others* v. *Ministro della Sanità* (1982) ECR 3415**

**Concerning: justification for refusal to make a reference to the ECJ under the Article 234 procedure**

### Facts

The facts of this case do not aid an understanding of the legal principle.

### Legal principle

This case considered whether there would be circumstances under which it would not be necessary to make a reference, even where there were questions of European law, and the matter was in a court of last instance. The court considered that it would not be necessary to make a reference where:

- The question of EC law is irrelevant
- The provision has already been interpreted by the ECJ
- The correct application of Community law is so obvious as to leave no room for reasonable doubt.

It would not be necessary under Article 234(3) to make a reference in such circumstances.

This case shows that it is still down to the national court to make the reference, and still within their power to find grounds on which to refuse to make a reference. The *CILFIT* criteria listed in the above case box are still rather strict, though, and therefore they serve to ensure that where the ECJ's opinion does not need to be sought, then the national court does not need to do so.

# ■ The *acte clair* principle

In certain circumstances, the national court may be justified in refusing to make a reference to the ECJ. This is of particular significance if the court would otherwise be considered to be a court of last instance under Article 234(3). Such a refusal may be justified under the principle of *acte clair*.

---

**KEY DEFINITION**

*Acte clair* This is a term borrowed from French administrative law. This phrase literally means that the law is clear or not in need of interpretation. If something is *acte clair*, then there is no reason to ask for clarification from the ECJ, and no question for the ECJ to answer.

---

The application of this principle can be seen through the cases. For example:

**KEY CASE**

**Case 28–30/62 *Da Costa en Schaake NV* v. *Nederlandse Belastingadministratie* (1963) ECR 31**

**Concerning: *acte clair***

**Facts**

This case concerned a request for a reference to the ECJ of questions which were virtually identical to those that had already been referred in the *van Gend en Loos* case, and therefore the national court had to decide whether it was appropriate to make a reference in this case too.

**Legal principle**

The court decided in this case that if a question is almost identical to one which had already been answered by the ECJ under the Article 234 procedure, then this will 'deprive the obligation [to refer] of its purpose and thus empty it of its substance.'

**KEY CASE**

**R v. Henn [1978] 1 WLR 1031**

**Concerning: application of *acte clair* principle**

**Facts**

This case concerned whether a ban on the import of pornographic materials was a quantitative restriction contrary to Article 28 of the EC Treaty. The court considered whether reference to the ECJ under Article 234 was necessary.

**Legal principle**

The Court of Appeal decided against making a reference, as previous ECJ case law suggested that this would not be a quantitative restriction under Article 28. However, when it reached the House of Lords, they did make a reference, and the ECJ decided that it *was* a quantitative restriction. The House of Lords warned about being too keen to decide that something was obvious, and therefore *acte clair*.

**EXAM TIP**

There is considerable overlap between the *CILFIT* criteria and the *acte clair* principle in their application, although it is important not to confuse the two. *Acte clair* is more straightforward, as it merely refers to an issue of obviousness, whereas the *CILFIT* criteria are more specific and also include the ability not to refer, even where it's a relevant question, but where it has already been answered before.

# Proceedings after the reference

Once the ECJ has answered the questions put to it under Article 234, the matter returns to the national court. It is important to bear in mind the following:

- The national court is under an obligation to follow the guidance of the ECJ and apply it to the case at hand (Member States have a general obligation under Article 10 of the EC Treaty to give effect to Community law in general – a broad obligation that covers this)
- The case must therefore still be active until the matter returns from the ECJ
- The national court applies the ruling to the facts. It is not the role of the ECJ to do this instead (see *Arsenal FC v. Reed* (2001) 2 CMLR 23).

**REVISION NOTE**

Remember: when it comes to applying the interpretation after the ECJ has dealt with the case, it is an issue of EU law that has been discussed. This is where questions on Article 234 overlap with other areas of **substantive** EU law. The free movement areas, or competition law, are good examples of where this can be the case. You would need to bring in your knowledge of these substantive areas alongside the procedure you have been discussing under Article 234.

# Chapter summary:
# Putting it all together

☐ Can you tick all the points from the revision checklist at the beginning of this chapter?

☐ Take the **end-of-chapter quiz** on the companion website.

☐ Test your knowledge of the cases below with the **revision flashcards** on the website.

☐ Attempt the essay question from the beginning of the chapter using the guidelines below.

☐ Go to the companion website to try out other questions.

## Answer guidelines

**See the essay question at the start of the chapter.**

This question asks you to consider the effectiveness of Article 234 as a cooperative procedure between the national courts and the ECJ, and its effectiveness in dealing with issues of Community law. It is a very open question, but allows you to demonstrate a clear and detailed understanding of this area of EU law.

It is important to:

■ be able to show an understanding of the Article 234 procedure, and the roles of the national court and the ECJ in it

■ discuss any conflicts between the ECJ and the national courts in relevant case law, in particular the problems encountered in the *Arsenal* case

■ discuss the advantages to the use of this system for the interpretation and application of EU law.

**Make your answer stand out**
This question is one which calls for more than mere reproduction of memorised facts about the Article 234 procedure, and therefore you need to use what you know about the procedure and issues raised by it to create an analytical discussion of the procedure and its purpose in the EU legal system.

## FURTHER READING

Saunders, O. (2004) 'A warning shot across the bows of the ECJ: The lessons of *Arsenal Football Club* v. *Reed*', Legal Executive Journal 38–40

Tridimas, T. (2003) 'Knocking on Heaven's Door: Fragmentation, Efficiency and Defiance in the Preliminary Reference Procedure', 40 Common Market Law Review 9–50

# 6
# Free movement of goods

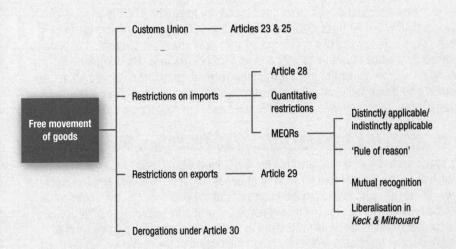

- Customs Union —— Articles 23 & 25
- Free movement of goods
  - Restrictions on imports
    - Article 28
    - Quantitative restrictions
    - MEQRs
      - Distinctly applicable/ indistinctly applicable
      - 'Rule of reason'
      - Mutual recognition
      - Liberalisation in *Keck & Mithouard*
  - Restrictions on exports —— Article 29
  - Derogations under Article 30

A printable version of this topic map is available from www.pearsoned.co.uk/lawexpress

# Revision Checklist

## Essential points you should know:

- [ ] The rules governing free movement of goods in the EU
- [ ] How those rules have evolved in the European Court of Justice
- [ ] The types of measures taken by national governments which will be prohibited by the rules
- [ ] How that applies to individual cases.

# Introduction:

Free movement of goods is central to the existence of the European Single Market. Without this freedom, an important part of the internal EU structure is missing. In order to achieve the free movement of goods, the EU has placed restrictions upon individual States' ability to tax or limit the movement of goods across national boundaries. The Treaty prohibits two types of border restrictions:

- those affecting imports of goods
- those affecting exports

where goods are being moved from one EU country to another. This is an area covered mainly by just three Treaty articles, Articles 28, 29 and 30, although there is a wealth of case law which has developed as a result of the ECJ's discussion of what is covered by the free movement rules, and what can be justified. This chapter will examine the development of the law from the Treaty through the cases, as often the issues to be discussed in an answer to either an essay-style question or a problem question require an understanding of the rules and how they have developed.

### Assessment advice

**Essay questions** An essay question on this subject would usually ask you to analyse the concept of free movement of goods through the cases, and therefore would require you to have a good knowledge of the relevant case law in this area. It may ask you to discuss the issues generally, or it may centre in on a particular issue, for example the Rule of Reason. In any event it will require some form of analysis, and therefore merely reiterating the history of the cases will not suffice.

### Assessment advice

**Problem questions** A problem question in this area is likely to be one which can overlap with other areas of EU law. For example, one common overlap can be with the Article 226 action, because if a Member State is in contravention of Article 28 or 29, this can also be the basis of an enforcement action by the European Commission under Article 226 (see Chapter 3). Alternatively the question may be one involving a company pursuing an action in the domestic courts, in which case there may also be issues of Direct Effects (see Chapter 1).

## Sample question

Could you answer this question? Below is a typical essay question that could arise on this topic. Guidelines on answering the question are included at the end of this chapter, whilst a sample problem question and guidance on tackling it can be found on the companion website.

### Essay question

Assess the importance the decision in Case 120/78 *Rewe-Zentral AG* v. *Bundesmonopolverwaltung für Branntwein (Cassis de Dijon)* (1979) ECR 649, and by reference to decided case law critically analyse the way in which the 'rule of reason' has subsequently been developed.

# ■ Free movement of goods under the EC Treaty

The principle of free movement of goods can be found in Articles 23–31 of the Treaty of Rome. However, this chapter concentrates on Articles 23, 25 and 28–30, as this is where the main focus of this area is, both in EU law courses and in assessments.

**KEY STATUTE**

### Article 23

'The Community shall be based upon a customs union which shall cover all trade in goods and which shall involve the prohibition between Member States of customs duties on imports and exports and of all charges having equivalent effect, and the adoption of a common customs tariff in their relations with third countries.'

| KEY DEFINITION |
| --- |

**Goods** are interpreted as 'products which can be valued in money and which are capable, as such, of forming the subject of commercial transactions'. (Case 7/68 *Re Export Tax on Art Treasures: EC Commission* v. *Italy* (1968) ECR 423 at 428).

The main provisions concerning free movement of goods are as follows:

| Treaty Article | Function |
| --- | --- |
| Article 25 | Prohibition on customs duties and charges having an equivalent effect |
| Article 28 | Elimination of quantitative restrictions on imports and measures having an equivalent effect (MEQRs) |
| Article 29 | Elimination of quantitative restrictions on exports and measures having an equivalent effect (MEQRs) |
| Article 30 | Derogations from Articles 28–29 |

# Article 25 – customs union

Article 25 provides a negative duty on the Member States not to impose customs duties. Member States need not take any action under this Article, but must not impose any new duties on imports and exports.

| KEY DEFINITION |
| --- |

**Negative duty** Many rules of EU law do not impose a duty to do something, but rather a duty NOT to do something – as seen here with Article 25, this is a negative duty.

For example, see:

**KEY CASE**

**Case 26/62 *Van Gend en Loos* v. *Nederlandse Administratie der Belastingen* (1963) ECR 1**

**Concerning: the imposition of an increased customs duty upon goods being imported into the Netherlands**

Facts

The goods in question here were reclassified by the Dutch government so they became subject to a higher rate of duty. The importers attempted to use Article 25 (formerly Article 12) to challenge the new duty in the national courts.

Legal principle

The ECJ ruled that the new duty was in contravention of Article 25, and that this Article provided a right which could be enforced by individual EU citizens.

# Article 28: restrictions on imports

However, the main area of controversy surrounds Articles 28–30.

**KEY STATUTE**

**Article 28**

Quantitative restrictions on imports and all measures having equivalent effect shall be prohibited between Member States.

**Problem area:** Treaty re-numbering and free movement of goods

With the renumbering that occurred under the Treaty of Amsterdam, Article 30 was renumbered Article 28 and Article 36 was re-numbered Article 30. Where cases refer to the old numbering system, this may cause confusion in this area, so please bear this in mind when reading cases decided before the Treaty of Amsterdam came into effect.

Unlike Article 25, Articles 28 and 29 required Member States to take positive action to make sure free movement of goods is respected, as well as refrain from taking action contrary to the principle.

Two types of measure are prohibited by Article 28:

▪ Quantitative restrictions on imports/exports
▪ Measures having an equivalent effect to quantitative restrictions (MEQRs).

# Quantitative restrictions

Quantitative restrictions are easily defined and therefore fairly uncontroversial. A quantitative restriction is one where imports or exports are either partially or totally restricted. This would include quota systems, bans, and also any form of licensing system. Even where the application for an import licence is considered a mere formality, it will still be considered a quantitative restriction because it is a mechanism whereby imports can be restricted. Quantitative restrictions often breach Article 28 merely because of their effect – they discriminate against imported products, and therefore attract the accusation that they are a barrier to free trade between EU Member States.

# MEQRs

MEQRs are wider in scope. They add complication to this area because they can be measures which apply to both domestic and imported products. However, it is their *effect* which is important. Although not defined by the Treaty, there are two definitions of MEQRs:

---

**KEY CASE**

**Case 8/74 *Procureur du Roi* v. *Dassonville* (1974) ECR 837 at 852**

**Concerning: definition of MEQR**

**Principle**

'All trading rules enacted by Member States which are capable of hindering, directly or indirectly, actually or potentially, intra-Community trade.'

---

**KEY STATUTE**

**Directive 70/50 Article 2(3) provides a non-exhaustive list of MEQRs, and subdivides them into:**

- Distinctly applicable measures (those which apply only to imported goods)
- Indistinctly applicable measures (those which apply equally to imported goods and domestically produced goods).

---

The definition in the *Dassonville* case was very broad, and therefore meant that a lot of actions of the Member States could breach Article 28, even where they resulted from national differences and were equally applicable to domestic products as they were to imports. The key in *Dassonville* was the potential for the EU to be re-divided along national borders by such measures. One major weakness of this definition is a lack of distinction between distinctly and indistinctly applicable measures.

# Distinctly applicable measures

These are measures which apply *only* to imports/exports or goods in transit. It is therefore more straightforward to assess whether they breach Articles 28 and 29, because in assessing their effect on the market, it is more straightforward to show that their effect is to discriminate in favour of domestic products.

# Indistinctly applicable measures

## KEY DEFINITION

**Indistinctly applicable measures** These are restrictions or other measures which apply equally to imported products and domestic products, for example Case 261/81 *Walter Rau Lebensmittelwerke* v. *De Smedt PVBA* (1982) ECR 3961, where there was a requirement in Belgium for all margarine sold there to be contained in cube-shaped boxes, or the *Cassis de Dijon* case (see below) where all cassis sold in Germany was required to contain at least 25% alcohol.

---

**KEY CASE**

**Case 120/78 *Rewe-Zentral AG* v. *Bundesmonopolverwaltung fur Branntwein (Cassis de Dijon)* (1979) ECR 649**

**Concerning: indistinctly applicable measures and their validity under Article 28**

Facts

A German law prohibited sale of various liquors (including cassis) in Germany with an alcohol content lower than 25%. The claimants in this case attempted to import French cassis into Germany, which had an alcohol content of somewhere between 15 and 20%.

Legal principle

The ECJ introduced two principles to address the problems caused by its previous failure in the *Dassonville* case to distinguish between distinctly applicable and indistinctly applicable measures. These would allow exceptions whereby indistinctly applicable measures would not be subject to Article 28 and therefore allow those indistinctly applicable measures to stand.

# The first *Cassis* rule: the Rule of Reason

Restrictions would be allowed for *indistinctly* applicable measures if they could satisfy certain mandatory requirements, such as:

- Effectiveness of fiscal supervision
- Protection of public health
- Fairness of consumer transactions
- Defence of the consumer.

Examples of this approach were discussed in the following cases:

| Case | Exception under the Rule of Reason |
|------|-----------------------------------|
| Cases 60 & 61/84 *Cinétheque SA* v. *Fédération Nationale des Cinémas Françaises* (1985) ECR 2605 | Protection of a Member State's culture |
| Case 302/86 *EC Commission* v. *Denmark* (1988) ECR 4607 | Protection of the environment |
| Case C-169/91 *Stoke-on-Trent City Council & Another* v. *B&Q Plc* (1993) 1 CMLR 426 | Socio-cultural characteristics of a country |
| Case 120/78 *Rewe-Zentral AG* v. *Bundesmonopolverwaltung fur Branntwein (Cassis de Dijon)* (1979) ECR 649 | Protection of public health |

The general rule appears to be that if a measure is necessary, then it can be allowed under the Rule of Reason. Necessary = proportionate, so for example, the ban in *Cassis* was not proportionate, as labelling would have been enough to protect the health of consumers, but the restriction in *Cinétheque* was proportionate.

| EXAM TIP |
|----------|
| Because the Rule of Reason does not provide an exhaustive list of examples of measures which would be allowed, the rule itself and the cases that followed it can only give examples of what has been permitted in the past. Therefore if you are faced with a problem question on this subject, the scenario could also be one which falls under the rule – but it is up to you to argue the case that it is proportionate. |

# The second *Cassis* rule: mutual recognition

Under the second rule in *Cassis*, provided the products have been lawfully introduced into one Member State, then there should be no reason why they should not be imported into another.

For example:

| Case | Example |
|------|---------|
| Case 16/83 *Criminal Proceedings Against Prantl* (1984) ECR 1299 | Import of Italian wine into Germany in bottles whose shape was normally restricted. This was allowed because the wine was legally marketed in Italy |
| Case 261/81 *Walter Rau Lebensmittelwerke* v. *De Smedt PVBA* (1982) ECR 3961 | Belgian law restricting margarine to cube-shaped tubs prohibited because margarine was lawfully sold in other types of packaging elsewhere in the EU |
| Case 178/84 *Commission* v. *Germany (Beer Purity Laws)* (1987) ECR 1227 | Beer from other EU states that did not comply with the German beer purity law could be imported and could be called beer because it was lawfully sold in other EU states |

## FURTHER THINKING

The decision in *Cassis de Dijon* highlighted an important issue concerning Article 28 – that the judgment in *Dassonville* was far too broad in its scope, and therefore there were some indistinctly applicable measures which should be excused despite being breaches of Article 28 under the *Dassonville* formula.

## FURTHER READING

Gormley, L.W. (1981) '*Cassis de Dijon* and the Communication from the Commission'
Weiler, J.J. (1999) 'From *Dassonville* to *Keck* and Beyond: An Evolutionary Reflection on the Text and Context of the Free Movement of Goods'

# The liberalisation of Article 28 and indistinctly applicable measures

KEY CASE

**Cases C-267 & C-268/91** *Keck & Mithouard* **(1993) ECR 1–6097**

**Concerning: indistinctly applicable measures under Article 28**

Facts

A French law prohibited the resale of goods that had not been altered or repackaged at a price lower than the price at which they had been bought, in order to prevent so-called 'predatory pricing' (the process of making a short-term loss in order to force competition out of the market).

The measure was challenged as being contrary to Article 28, and the ECJ modified its approach to indistinctly applicable measures on the grounds that traders had increasingly used these laws to challenge limits to their commercial freedom.

Legal principle

Where a measure was indistinctly applicable, if that measure constituted a 'selling arrangement', then it would not breach Article 28.

The phrase 'selling arrangement' has not been clearly defined. There are, however, cases which have distinguished between selling arrangements and other product-related requirements, with the latter falling outside the principle in *Keck*.

| Selling arrangements | Other product-related requirements to be met |
|---|---|
| Case C-292/92 *Hünermund*: prohibition on pharmacies advertising certain pharmaceutical products outside their premises<br>Case C-412/93 *Leclerc-Siplec*: prohibition on television advertising for certain products | Case C-470/93 *Mars*: prohibition on certain advertising claims on packaging<br>Case C-366/04 *Schwarz*: requirement to individually package chewing gum dispensed by a vending machine |

## FURTHER THINKING

The *Keck* case at first glance appears to be doing nothing more than further splitting indistinctly applicable measures into two further sub-groups; however, the case was significant in that it halted the advanced use of Article 28 by traders where they were challenging national rules only because they limited their commercial freedom. For example, see the Sunday trading cases in the UK for examples of where DIY retailers were using European law to directly challenge the Sunday trading rules in the UK:

Case C-145/88 *Torfaen Borough Council* v. *B&Q Plc* (1989) ECR 3851
Case C-169/91 *Stoke-on-Trent City Council* v. *B&Q Plc* (1992) ECR I-6635
*Wellingborough Borough Council* v. *Payless DIY Ltd* (1990) 1 CMLR 773

*Keck* was therefore further refining the rules concerning national differences and creating a situation whereby such differences were not to be removed just because the rules in one country were stricter than in others.

## FURTHER READING

Chalmers, D. (1994) 'Repackaging the Internal Market – the Ramifications of the Keck Judgement', 19 European Law Review 385–403
Gormley, L. (1994) 'Reasoning Renounced? The Remarkable Judgement in Keck and Mithouard', European Business Law Review 63–67

## EXAM TIP

The three cases of *Dassonville*, *Cassis de Dijon* and *Keck & Mithouard* form the basis of the development of the law in the area of Article 28. It is therefore essential that these cases form part of your revision in this area – not only will they help you to understand how this area has evolved, but it will also demonstrate to the examiner that you have an understanding of how Article 28 has been applied to the cases. The rest of the case law should also form part of your revision, but you will find it more straightforward if you use these three cases as your starting point.

# Article 29: restrictions on exports

**KEY STATUTE**

**Article 29**

Quantitative restrictions on exports, and all measures having equivalent effect, shall be prohibited between Member States.

## Figure 6.1

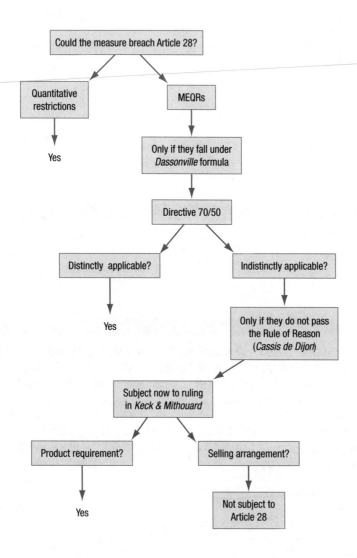

Unlike Article 28 (see Fig. 6.1), there are no indistinctly applicable measures, and the *Dassonville* test does not apply. A measure has to have as its specific object the restriction of intra-Community trade (that is, trade between Member States), and therefore it is a lot more difficult to argue this than with Article 28. Only measures which can be shown to be protectionist will breach Article 29.

# Article 30: derogations from Articles 28 and 29

## KEY STATUTE

### Article 30

The provisions of Articles 28 and 29 shall not preclude prohibitions or restrictions on imports, exports or goods in transit justified on grounds of public morality, public policy or public security; the protection of health and life of humans, animals or plants; the protection of national treasures possessing artistic, historical or archaeological value; or the protection of industrial and commercial property. Such prohibitions or restrictions shall not, however, constitute a means of arbitrary discrimination or a disguised restriction on trade between Member States.

Article 30 provides situations where Member States may be excused something which is a restriction of Article 28 or 29. However:

- The list in Article 30 is *exhaustive*
- Proven ulterior motives can prevent a restriction being justified under Article 30
- Where rules have been harmonised at Community level, then a measure may not be justified under Article 30
- Provisions are narrowly construed and must satisfy the test of proportionality.

Examples of each of the areas on the list are as follows:

| Article 30 justification | Case |
|---|---|
| Public morality | Compare:<br>*R* v. *Henn & Darby* (justified prohibition on pornography due to illegality in the UK)<br>with:<br>*Conegate* v. *Customs & Excise* (prohibition not justified as products were not prohibited in UK) |
| Public policy | *R* v. *Thompson* (restriction on export of collector's coins justified because of the need to protect mint coinage) |
| Public security | Case 72/83 *Campus Oil Ltd* (requirement for importers of petroleum to buy 35% of their products from the nationalised refinery allowed Ireland to maintain the ability to refine petroleum, an important security consideration) |
| Protection of life or health of humans, animals and plants | Case 4/75 *Rewe-Zentralfinanz GmbH* v. *Landwirtschaftskammer* (1975) ECR 843 (inspection requirement which only applied to imported apples was justified because of the real risk to health from something which was not present in domestic apples) |
| Protection of national treasures possessing artistic, historic or archaeological value | Case 7/68 *Re Export Tax on Art Treasures* (1968) ECR 423 (quantitative restriction on export of art treasures was justified, but a tax was not) |
| Protection of industrial and commercial property | Case 78/70 *Deutsche Grammophon Gesellschaft mbH* v. *Metro-SB-Grossmarkte GmbH* (1971) ECR 487 |

# Chapter summary:
# Putting it all together

## TEST YOURSELF

☐ Can you tick all the points from the revision checklist at the beginning of this chapter?

☐ Take the **end-of-chapter quiz** on the companion website.

☐ Test your knowledge of the cases below with the **revision flashcards** on the website.

☐ Attempt the essay question from the beginning of the chapter using the guidelines below.

☐ Go to the companion website to try out other questions.

## Answer guidelines

**See the essay question at the start of the chapter. A diagram illustrating how to structure your answer is available on the website.**

This question asks you specifically to examine the *Cassis de Dijon* case, but within the context of the law on free movement of goods, and including a discussion of how the law has developed since then. Just because the *Cassis* case is the one mentioned does not mean that this is the only case law that needs to be discussed – this question would allow you to demonstrate your understanding of the area as a whole, through a discussion of this case's place in that. You should therefore be prepared to discuss cases both before and after this judgment. An approach to this question could include the following points:

■ An introduction summarising the area of law and pointing out the important issues to be discussed in your answer; in this case, it will be centred on Article 28

■ A discussion of the issues raised by the inclusion of indistinctly applicable and distinctly applicable measures under Article 28

■ An assessment of the importance of the *Cassis* case, including a discussion of:
  – The decision made in the case itself
  – The issues raised by that decision which are of more general application

■ An evaluation of how that decision may have changed the law in the area, and the significance of that change

■ The cases which have followed on from *Cassis*, and how they may have changed the application of *Cassis* in EU law today

■ A conclusion which summarises the issues and the relevance of the *Keck* decision to current application of EU law.

**Make your answer stand out**
Where you are asked to answer an essay question where a specific case is mentioned in the title, there is often the temptation to write everything and anything you know about that case without thought as to structure or as to how that is going to answer the question. It is important that an answer to a question of this type has a clear structure, and that you see through the case to the context in which the case sits, and are able to use the case to critically evaluate the area of law in question. Being able to produce a meaningful discussion using the case and related cases will make your answer stand out.

## FURTHER READING

Chalmers, D. (1994) 'Repackaging the Internal Market – the Ramifications of the Keck Judgement', 19 European Law Review 385

Gormley, L.W. (1981) '*Cassis de Dijon* and the Communication from the Commission', 6 EL Rev 454

Gormley, L.W. (1994) 'Reasoning Renounced? The Remarkable Judgement in *Keck and Mithouard*', European Business Law Review 63

Steiner, J. (1992) 'Drawing the Line: Uses and Abuses of Article 30 EEC', 29 Common Market Law Review 749

Weatherill, S. (1996) 'After *Keck*: Some Thoughts on how to Clarify the Clarification', 33 Common Market Law Review 885

Weiler, J.J. (1999) 'From *Dassonville* to *Keck* and Beyond: An Evolutionary Reflection on the Text and Context of the Free Movement of Goods', in P. Craig and G. de Burca (eds.) *The Evolution of EU Law*, Oxford University Press, chapter 10

# 7
# Free movement of workers

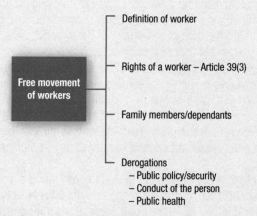

Free movement of workers
- Definition of worker
- Rights of a worker – Article 39(3)
- Family members/dependants
- Derogations
  - Public policy/security
  - Conduct of the person
  - Public health

A printable version of this topic map is available from www.pearsoned.co.uk/lawexpress

# Revision Checklist

## Essential points you should know:

- [ ] The basis and purpose of free movement of workers and their families within the EU
- [ ] The rules concerning the right of an EU citizen to move freely within the EU for work
- [ ] Any restrictions upon that freedom of movement and their purpose
- [ ] Rules covering the freedom of movement of family or dependants of a worker.

# Introduction:

Free movement of workers is one of the fundamental freedoms of the Single European Market. It was originally established to complement the other freedoms (goods, capital, services) and therefore promote economic activity within the Community, but can also be seen as an important right for individuals who are EU citizens, to allow them and their families to move freely throughout the Community without restrictions. Through Directive 2004/38, the concept is gradually being transformed into a more general one of citizenship, which works through consideration of other freedoms alongside this one. However, economic activity of persons moving around the EU remains one of the most important aspects of this. The aim of this chapter is to review the rules concerning freedom of movement of persons classed specifically as 'workers', although a broader concept of free movement of persons can be seen if you consider free movement of services too. Some of the secondary legislation does not distinguish between employed persons and self-employed persons (who are dealt with through the rules concerning 'establishment'). We will also be examining the situations in which a person may bring their family or dependants along when migrating between Member States, and any restrictions that the Member States are allowed to impose upon individuals attempting to move between Member States for work.

Where this area is assessed, it can appear in exam questions as a discrete subject of itself, but as with most EU law, can also overlap into other areas. It is not a complex area of EU law, and you can get a good grasp of the principles through an appreciation of how the law applies to everyday life in the EU.

**Assessment advice**

Questions in this area generally take the form of scenario-based problem questions. A question will usually involve a situation covering a person and their family either working or attempting to work in a Member State other than their own, and the application of the rules to their situation. It is most important to be familiar with the concept of 'worker' under the Treaty and relevant secondary legislation, along with the derogations and how they may be applied to the worker. The status of family members may also be raised as an issue in a problem question, so it is important to be familiar with the rules concerning which family members are also entitled to residence as dependants of the worker.

## Sample question

Could you answer this question? Below is a typical problem question that could arise on this topic. Guidelines on answering the question are included at the end of this chapter, whilst a sample essay question and guidance on tackling it can be found on the companion website.

**Problem question**

Stefan, a Danish national, and Juanita, a Portuguese national, have been living together for three years in Denmark. They decide to try and work in the UK, and move to Manchester for this purpose.

After trying to find work for three months without success, Juanita gives up and decides to enrol at the local college in order to study fashion design. Her application for financial assistance is refused as she is not a national of the country. She invites her Brazillian grandmother, Tatiana, to stay with them in Manchester, but on her arrival in the UK, Tatiana is refused entry.

Stefan, in the meantime, has found part-time work as a parcel courier, but Juanita is asked to leave the country, as she and Stefan are not married. Further, Stefan's employer is suspected of using his business to cover a drug smuggling ring, and as a result, Stefan is rounded up by the police and recommended for deportation as 'undesirable'.

**Advise Stefan, Juanita and Tatiana of their rights in EC law.**

# ■ Free movement of workers under the EC Treaty

The concept of free movement of workers is enshrined in the Treaty as one of the four fundamental freedoms. The freedom itself is contained in Articles 39 and 40 of the Treaty, along with the powers given to the EU to make secondary legislation on the matter.

KEY STATUTE

**Article 39 EC**

1 Freedom of movement for workers shall be secured within the Community.
2 Such freedom of movement shall entail the abolition of any discrimination based on nationality between workers of the Member States as regards employment, remuneration and other conditions of work and employment.

This Article makes three important points:

■ A worker is entitled to move freely throughout the Community for the purposes of getting a job and performing that job (Art 39(1) and (3));
■ A worker has the right not to be discriminated against based on his/her nationality (Art 39(2));
■ That right is subject to several exceptions (Art 39(2) and (4)).

This Article, however, does not contain a lot of detail concerning how this is to be put into practice (it does not even define 'worker', for example) and therefore there is a right contained in Article 40 giving the EU the right to make secondary legislation in order to provide the detail needed.

# Free movement of workers under secondary legislation

Free movement of workers is primarily dealt with through the secondary legislation, Regulation 1612/68, and Directive 2004/38. The role of these pieces of legislation is to provide the detail that the EC Treaty does not provide.

# Definition of 'worker'

When dealing with this area, the first thing you must establish is that the person concerned is classed as a worker. In most circumstances, this will be a fairly straightforward question, although in some cases the answer is not as obvious as appears. If we start from basic principles, a worker can be defined as follows:

### KEY DEFINITION

**Worker** A worker is an EU national who is either in employment (full or part time) in that he/she is paid in return for his/her performance under an employer/employee relationship, or is seeking actual paid work.

This definition does not come from the Treaty, but can be explained by the case law surrounding this area. Article 39 failed to define what a worker was, and therefore the ECJ has taken a broad approach to defining 'worker' through the case law. Below are some examples of decisions from the ECJ on the definition of 'worker', but first, the *Lawrie-Blum* case provides a general explanation.

> **KEY CASE**
>
> **Case 66/85 *Lawrie-Blum* v. *Land Baden-Württemburg* (1986) ECR 2121**
>
> **Concerning: definition of 'worker' under Article 39**
>
> **Facts**
>
> This case concerned a trainee teacher in Germany. The German government attempted to argue that Lawrie-Blum was not a 'worker' because of his trainee status.
>
> **Legal principle**
>
> The ECJ found that the trainee teacher was a 'worker,' and set out a three-part test to deal with the issue. They defined a worker as someone who:
>
> 1 during a certain period of time
> 2 performs services for and under the direction of another
> 3 in return for remuneration.

Other case law has also taken this broad approach to defining a worker. The concept of worker has two parts, an economic part and a formal part.

# Economic aspect of 'worker'

A worker has to be performing duties in exchange for some economic gain, whether that be money or otherwise. The Table gives examples of how the courts have dealt with the economic part of this.

| Case | Principle |
| --- | --- |
| Case 53/81 *Levin* v. *Staatssecretaris van Justitie* (1982) ECR 1035 | The definition of worker included those doing part-time work |
| Case 196/87 *Steymann* v. *Staatssecretaris van Justitie* (1988) ECR 6159 | Payment for work did not have to be monetary, but could be a benefit in kind |
| Case 139/85 *Kempf* v. *Staatssecretaris van Justitie* (1986) ECR 1741 | Someone who does not earn enough to live on (and therefore must also claim benefits) is still a worker |

# Formal aspect of 'worker'

On the formal aspect, a worker must be someone defined as 'employed'. Therefore, you would expect an employer/employee relationship to exist, with the employee taking instructions from the employer.

| Case | Principle |
|------|-----------|
| Case 66/85 *Lawrie-Blum* v. *Land Baden-Württemburg* (1986) ECR 2121 | Someone who performs a service under the direction of another |
| Case 75/63 *Hoekstra* v. *BBDA* (191964) ECR 177 | A worker could also be someone who had recently lost their job, and was looking to take another one |

# Working and seeking work

Because often it is necessary to enter a Member State in order to get work, those looking for work are treated in a similar fashion to workers, but only for a limited time:

**KEY CASE**

**Case C-292/89 *R* v. *Immigration Appeal Tribunal ex parte Antonissen* (1991) ECR I-745**

**Concerning: status as 'worker' when seeking work in another Member State**

**Facts**

Antonissen was appealing against a decision to deport him, claiming free movement as a worker under Article 48 (now 39) as he had been looking for work in the UK. However, he had not found any for over six months.

**Legal principle**

The ECJ held that it was reasonable for the Member State to deport someone if they had not found work within six months.

Article 6 of Directive 2004/38 allows any EU national to remain in any Member State for up to three months without having to conform to the definition of 'worker', but beyond this, unless there is a realistic chance of them getting a job, they can be required to leave the State concerned.

The simple answer to the issue of seeking work is to apply a time limit of three months, because from Directive 2004/38, this appears to be a reasonable conclusion to come to. However, this is a grey area, because if a person can show that he/she is **seeking** employment, and has a realistic chance of getting a job, then they may be able to show they have a right to stay, even though the three months has expired. Deeper thinking like this will enable you to show a better understanding of the subject when tackling an exam question. The point about the time limit was emphasised in Case C-138/02 *Brian Francis Collins* v. *Secretary of State for Work and Pensions* (2004) ECR I-2703, so in theory a person could stay in a Member State a lot longer, although the Member State is allowed to lay down a reasonable time limit for this.

# Rights of a worker

**KEY STATUTE**

### Article 39(3)

3 It shall entail the right, subject to limitations justified on grounds of public policy, public security or public health:
 (a) to accept offers of employment actually made;
 (b) to move freely within the territory of Member States for this purpose;
 (c) to stay in a Member State for the purpose of employment in accordance with the provisions governing the employment of nationals of that State laid down by law, regulation or administrative action;
 (d) to remain in the territory of a Member State after having been employed in that State, subject to conditions which shall be embodied in implementing regulations to be drawn up by the Commission.

The rights outlined above are dealt with generally by Directive 2004/38. All rights concerning movement into or out of a Member State are subject to the need to have a valid passport. In summary, the most important of these rights are:

| Right | Source |
|-------|--------|
| Right to enter | Article 5(1) Directive 2004/38 |
| Right to leave | Article 4(1) Directive 2004/38 |
| Right to reside | ▋ Without a job (up to three months): Article 6 Directive 2004/38<br>▋ With a job: Article 7 Directive 2004/38 |
| Right to remain after losing a job | Article 7(3) Directive 2004/38, if:<br>▋ Temporarily unable to work because of illness<br>▋ Involuntarily unemployed and seeking work<br>▋ Started vocational training |
| Right of permanent residence | Article 16(1) Directive 2004/38 after continuous residence of five years |

## Public sector work

Jobs in the public sector are specifically excluded under Article 39(4). It is important for the government of a country to restrict certain public sector jobs to their own nationals.

## Non-discrimination under Article 39(2)

**KEY STATUTE**

**Article 39(2)**

Such freedom of movement shall entail the abolition of any discrimination based on nationality between workers of the Member States as regards employment, remuneration and other conditions of work and employment.

Regulation 1612/68 outlaws many obstacles to migrant workers in its first 12 Articles. This therefore means that a worker is allowed access to the same jobs, tax and social advantages as if he were a national of that country. However, Member States are justified in withholding social assistance (including financial) during the first three months of the worker's residence. (See Article 24(2) of Directive 2004/38.) They can also withhold any financial support for training or studying until the worker has permanent residence rights.

# ■ Rights of family members and dependants

When a worker moves within the Single Market, of course his family and dependants will need to move as well. The Treaty does not mention family members. However, Article 2(2) Directive 2004/38 gives details of family members and dependants who have the right to move into the Member State with the worker (Fig. 7.1).

**Figure 7.1**

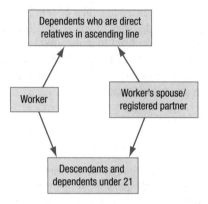

**Problem area:** Descendants and dependants under 21

It is important to note that children of either the worker or his/her spouse have particularly special status: the term 'children' includes all children of either partner, not just those who are common to both the worker and their partner. They also remain part of the worker's family, even after a divorce has taken place. They are also protected by Article 8 of the European Convention on Human Rights, which protects the right to family life. Article 12 Directive 2004/38 also gives them the same right to education as nationals of that State.

## FURTHER THINKING

The situation concerning family members can become complicated – because their status will be dependent upon the status of the worker, and in this way they can be disadvantaged. See Woods, L. (1999) 'Family Rights in the EU – Disadvantaging the Disadvantaged?', 11 Child & Family Law Quarterly 17

# ■ Derogations from free movement of workers

| KEY DEFINITION |
|---|

**Derogation** The exemption from, or the relaxation of, a particular law. In this context, exceptions to the rule requiring free movement for workers.

The right of free movement for workers is not absolute – you also have to bear in mind that there are some circumstances in which a Member State can either refuse entry to a worker, or require them to leave. If you look at Article 39(3), it refers to the rights of a worker being generally 'subject to limitations justified on grounds of public policy, public security or public health'. This is quite a vague phrase, and Directive 2004/38 deals with specifics of how it is to be applied. It is possible to see its influence in refining these quite general concepts.

## Public policy and public security

The public policy ground for excluding migrant workers is probably the vaguest of the three derogations, and therefore potentially most open to abuse by a Member State that wants to justify excluding someone. Public security is also generally considered at the same time, as the two concepts overlap. The ECJ's approach has been to give it a very narrow meaning. Have a look at the evolution of this concept in the Table below.

| Case/Article | Meaning of 'public policy' |
|---|---|
| Case 41/74 *van Duyn* v. *Home Office* (1974) ECR 1337 | Activities/membership of an organisation considered to be 'socially harmful' |
| Case 30/77 *R* v. *Bouchereau* (1977) ECR 1999 | Activities which are a genuine and sufficiently serious threat to the requirements of public policy affecting one of the fundamental interests of society |
| Article 27(2) Directive 2004/38 | 'Must represent a genuine, present and sufficiently serious threat affecting one of the fundamental interests of society' |

There are also several other considerations under Directive 2004/38. Member States are not allowed to use the public policy derogation in the following circumstances:

| Article | Exception |
|---------|-----------|
| Article 15(2) | Not having a passport or ID card is not grounds for expelling a person |
| Article 27(1) | Prohibits excluding a person for economic purposes |
| Article 27(2) | Previous criminal convictions on their own are not enough to exclude a person |

# Conduct of the person

A reason for excluding someone under public policy or public security has to be based on the conduct or behaviour of the person concerned – see Article 27(2) of Directive 2004/38. The important factor to remember is that the behaviour or activity of that person must be current, and not merely something in that person's past. Here are some examples:

**KEY CASE**

**Case 41/74 *Van Duyn* v. *Home Office* (1974) ECR 1337**

**Concerning: exclusion of a migrant worker on grounds of public policy based upon association with a particular group**

Facts

Van Duyn was a Dutch woman who wanted to enter the UK to take up a job working within the Church of Scientology in the UK. Although not a banned organisation, it was viewed by the UK government as undesirable. The Home Office refused her entry on grounds that her conduct, as a member of this organisation, was contrary to public policy.

Legal principle

The ECJ decided that the concept of public policy had to be interpreted narrowly, but that a Member State had a certain amount of discretion as to how it was to be applied. Therefore van Duyn's *current* membership of this organisation could constitute grounds for refusing her entry, even where it was not a banned organisation. The activity has to be considered 'socially harmful'.

**KEY CASE**

## Case 30/77 *R* v. *Bouchereau* (1977) ECR 1999

### Concerning: criminal convictions as 'conduct' under public policy grounds for exclusion

#### Facts

Mr. Bouchereau was a Frenchman who had been convicted on several occasions of drug possession. Because of his convictions, the UK were attempting to expel him, and claimed they were justified in doing so because of his conduct.

#### Legal principle

The activities of the person concerned must be socially harmful in order to justify expelling him.

---

### EXAM TIP

The important point of the above case is that it's not just a history of criminal convictions that allows a person to be expelled – the longer the time since the conviction, the less likely it is to be relevant. Therefore, it is important to weigh up the seriousness of the criminal offence and how long ago it was committed if faced with a scenario that includes a person with a criminal record.

---

**KEY CASE**

## Case 67/74 *Bonsignore* v. *Oberstadtdirektor of the City of Cologne* (1975) ECR 297

### Concerning: expulsion under public security used preventatively

#### Facts

Bonsignore was an Italian working in Germany. He was convicted of a minor firearms offence and the German government attempted to deport him back to Italy. They claimed it was in order to deter other immigrants from committing similar offences.

#### Legal principle

The argument was rejected. The ECJ said that the reason had to be about the possible future behaviour of that person, not in order generally to prevent others from following his example.

# Public health

This has a broader scope than the other two derogations here. According to Article 29, it is limited to the following:

- 'diseases with epidemic potential'
- 'other infectious diseases or contagious parasitic diseases'.

The important thing here is that this is also limited in time (unlike the other two derogations). If a disease is contracted more than three months after the worker has entered the country, then it cannot be a reason for expelling him. Also, HIV/AIDS is excepted – the free movement of persons with this disease is guaranteed by a communication from the European Commission.

# Chapter summary:
# Putting it all together

**TEST YOURSELF**

☐ Can you tick all the points from the revision checklist at the beginning of this chapter?

☐ Take the **end-of-chapter quiz** on the companion website.

☐ Test your knowledge of the cases below with the **revision flashcards** on the website.

☐ Attempt the problem question from the beginning of the chapter using the guidelines below.

☐ Go to the companion website to try out other questions.

## Answer guidelines

**See the problem question at the start of the chapter.**

This question requires you to consider the rights of three individuals, two of whom are EU nationals while the other is not. You must first consider the rights of the two EU nationals, and then any that the non-EU national may have in relation to them.
   Consider:

■ Stefan and Juanita are entitled to live in the UK for up to three months looking for work (Article 6 Directive 2004/38).

■ Stefan has found a job – but it is part-time – does this allow him to be classed as a worker? See *Levin*.

■ Juanita has not found work; can she still be classed as a 'worker'? Consider whether she is entitled to any support in relation to her education under Directive 2004/38 either as a worker, or as part of Stefan's 'family'. Also, consider whether she is entitled to remain in the country either as a 'worker' or as part of Stefan's 'family'. Can she say she is actively seeking work?

■ Tatiana is not an EU national, and therefore does not have any rights of free movement as a worker, but is she part of the family of a worker? See Article 2(2) of Directive 2004/38.

■ Can Stefan be deported merely for his association with a suspected drug trafficker? Look at public policy grounds for derogation from free movement of workers under Article 39(2).

**Make your answer stand out**
You must consider the way in which the ECJ has approached the application of these rules, and not just the rules themselves. A good answer to this question will consider

the broad or narrow interpretation placed upon the rights and exceptions in this area in order to provide an accurate application of the law to the facts, which should result in clear advice to the parties concerned.

### FURTHER READING

Castro Oliveira, A. (2002) 'Workers and Other Persons: Step-by-step from movement to citizenship', 39 CML Rev 77

Dougan, M. (2005) 'Fees, Grants, Loans and Dole Cheques: Who covers the cost of migrant education within the EU?', 42 CML Rev 943

Woods, L. (1999) 'Family Rights in the EU – Disadvantaging the Disadvantaged?', 11 Child & Family Law Quarterly 17

# 8
# Competition law

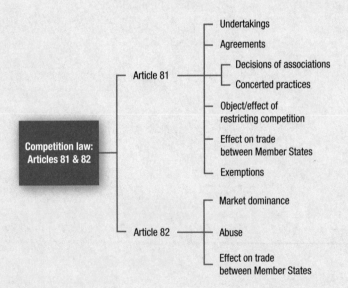

- Article 81
  - Undertakings
  - Agreements
    - Decisions of associations
    - Concerted practices
  - Object/effect of restricting competition
  - Effect on trade between Member States
  - Exemptions

- Competition law: Articles 81 & 82

- Article 82
  - Market dominance
  - Abuse
  - Effect on trade between Member States

A printable version of this topic map is available from www.pearsoned.co.uk/lawexpress

# Revision Checklist

## Essential points you should know:

- [ ] The purpose behind the use of Articles 81 and 82 to regulate competition law in Europe
- [ ] The definitions applied in the Treaty to both Articles 81 and 82
- [ ] The way in which Article 81 is applied to anti-competitive agreements
- [ ] The application of exemptions to Article 81, such as block exemptions and comfort letters
- [ ] The application of Article 82 to anti-competitive abuses of a dominant position.

## Introduction:

Competition law in Articles 81 and 82 is just one aspect of the rules set up by the EU to regulate the Single Market. The aim is to ensure that there is as free a market as possible, but with enough regulation to ensure that the market is not abused. Articles 81 and 82 are therefore only a part of this, but a key part. These two treaty articles prohibit:

- anti-competitive agreements between *undertakings* and restrictive practices
- abuse by a company of a dominant position in the market.

When looking at these rules, it is important to note the context within which they sit: they are part of the measures aimed at the smooth running of the Single European Market, and you should also bear in mind that there are rules for Member States to follow (regarding free movement and the customs union) and also anti-dumping measures, and so although an examination question may not cover all these areas, you should always bear in mind that Articles 81 and 82 exist in this wider context.

The aim of this chapter is to examine the rules in Articles 81 and 82, and look at how they have been applied in practice through the case law. This should therefore allow you to consider the use of these rules in a practical context (useful for problem questions) and also the more theoretical aspects (useful for essay questions).

### Assessment advice

Questions on this area of law can vary according to the way in which competition law is taught at your university, as the focus of the subject can vary greatly. Problem questions are probably the most straightforward to deal with, as they will be looking for the application of the law to the scenario outlined in the question. As EU competition law is heavily based on the criteria in Articles 81 and 82, this can be a fairly straightforward exercise if you are also prepared to discuss a range of cases that help to illustrate the application of these principles. Essay questions will also call for knowledge of the cases, as the question will require knowledge of this area beyond the rules and definitions in the Treaty.

# Sample question

Could you answer this question? Below is a typical essay question that could arise on this topic. Guidelines on answering the question are included at the end of this chapter, whilst a sample problem question and guidance on tackling it can be found on the companion website.

**Essay question**

Critically evaluate the effect of the introduction of Regulation 1/2003 on Article 81. Does the new system under this Regulation have any advantages beyond merely reducing the workload of the Commission in granting individual exemptions?

# ■ Article 81: anti-competitive agreements between undertakings

**KEY STATUTE**

**Articles 81(1) and 81(2)**

1  The following shall be prohibited as incompatible with the common market: all agreements between undertakings, decisions by associations of undertakings and concerted practices which may affect trade between Member States and which have as their object or effect the prevention, restriction or distortion of competition within the common market, and in particular those which:

   (a)  directly or indirectly fix purchase or selling prices or any other trading conditions;

   (b)  limit or control production, markets, technical development, or investment;

   (c)  share markets or sources of supply;

   (d)  apply dissimilar conditions to equivalent transactions with other trading parties, thereby placing them at a competitive disadvantage;

   (e)  make the conclusion of contracts subject to acceptance by the other parties of supplementary obligations which, by their nature or according to commercial usage, have no connection with the subject of such contracts.

2  Any agreements or decisions prohibited pursuant to this Article shall be automatically void.

**Figure 8.1**

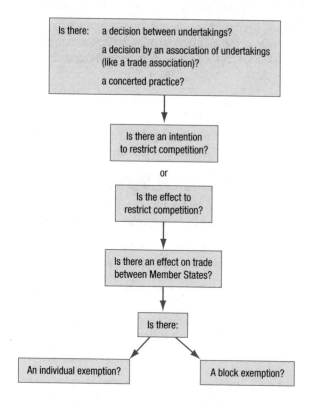

Article 81's purpose is to prevent any restrictive practices which may have an effect on competition in the EU (Fig. 8.1). It is very specific about the type of activities it includes (those listed under (a) to (e) in the quote from Article 81 above), although this list is not exhaustive. In order to understand Article 81, you need to break it down into its different parts.

## Who does Article 81 apply to?

Article 81 is aimed at private bodies, or 'undertakings' as it says in the Treaty. It is **not** there to deal with the activities of governments or the public sector – they are dealt with by other parts of the Treaty.

COMPETITION LAW

## KEY DEFINITION

**Undertakings** This is intended to cover only private individuals, and so it means natural persons (such as you and I) or legal persons (companies). However, in the context of Article 81, it has also been defined as groups of companies too.

# What does Article 81 prohibit?

There are three broad categories of what it prohibits: 'agreements between undertakings, decisions by associations of undertakings and concerted practices'.

| Activity | Meaning |
|---|---|
| Agreements between undertakings | Can be both binding/non-binding, written or verbal. Can even include 'gentlemen's agreements' |
| Decisions by associations of undertakings | Binding or non-binding instructions/recommendations by trade associations to members |
| Concerted practices | Action by competitors in a market arising from them coordinating their actions, such as coordinated price rises by different companies where there is no other plausible explanation other than the concerted practice |

This means that Article 81 can have a broad coverage. Although in the first two examples there has to be evidence of an agreement in place, the idea of concerted practices is a lot wider, although it is still down to the Commission to get evidence to show that what is happening is a concerted practice, and not just everyone raising their prices when one company does, as happens with petrol prices.

**KEY CASE**

## Case 11, 40–8, 50, 56, 113–4/73 *Suiker Unie* v. *Commission* (1975) ECR 1663

### Concerning: meaning of 'concerted practice'

### Facts

Sugar producers in the EU had decided only to import into Holland with permission from the main Dutch producers. Doing this meant that there was less pressure on the Dutch sugar producers to compete than there would have been had the other producers just imported into the country without their permission. They were accused of engaging in a concerted practice, but claimed they were not because there was no agreement between the different sugar producers to do this.

### Legal principle

The ECJ held that it was not necessary for there to be a specific understanding in order for this to be a concerted practice. It just needed to involve some sort of contact, whether it be direct or indirect, which led to the action (like price-fixing) taking place. A concerted practice allows competitors to fix a position in the knowledge of what others are going to do.

## Object or effect of restricting competition

In some situations it is possible to show that there was intention to restrict competition, but even if this is not the case, then if it can be shown that the effect (whether intended or not) was to restrict competition, then this will be enough.

**EXAM TIP**

Remember when looking at this issue that if you are dealing with a problem question, you need to look at the effect *within the relevant market*, so it is important to be able to define the relevant product market, or the relevant geographical area.

There are also two types of agreement that can have an effect on the relevant market, and Article 81 applies to both of them:

| Type of agreement | Definition |
|---|---|
| Vertical agreements | Between those on different levels, e.g. imposed upon a distributor by the supplier |
| Horizontal agreements | Between firms that operate on the same level in the market |

KEY CASE

## Case 56&58/64 *Consten* v. *Commission* (1966) ECR 299

### Concerning: types of agreements covered by Article 81

#### Facts

This case concerned an agreement between a supplier and their distributor for products to be sold in France. An agreement was made between them that the distributor would not sell outside France, and in return the supplier agreed to make agreements with its other European distributors that they would not sell in France. The agreement was challenged under Article 81 when another distributor (from Germany) started selling the products in France at a lower price.

#### Legal principle

The ECJ decided that the agreement was contrary to Article 81, and in doing so, it made several important points:

- Article 81 could apply to vertical agreements (as this one was) as well as horizontal ones
- The fact that this agreement had streamlined and increased distribution of the product in question was irrelevant
- The important point here was that the agreement had harmed the Single European Market by an attempt to repartition along national boundaries.

# Examples of what is prohibited in Article 81(1)

The list in Article 81(1) is not meant to be exclusive – there are other things which potentially could breach Article 81 *if* they meet the criteria discussed above. However, they are a good starting point. They are as follows:

(a) directly or indirectly fix purchase or selling prices or any other trading conditions;
(b) limit or control production, markets, technical development, or investment;
(c) share markets or sources of supply;
(d) apply dissimilar conditions to equivalent transactions with other trading parties, thereby placing them at a competitive disadvantage;
(e) make the conclusion of contracts subject to acceptance by the other parties of supplementary obligations which, by their nature or according to commercial usage, have no connection with the subject of such contracts.

# Effect on trade between Member States

**Problem area:** *de minimis*

Both Articles 81 and 82 deal with activities that may affect free competition within the EU. However, not all agreements or abuses may be subject to this rule. Have a look at Case 5/69 *Volk v Vervaecke* (1969) ECR 295, where it was decided that the agreement didn't breach Article 81 because it didn't have a significant effect on the market. However, in Case 23/67 *Brasserie de Haecht v Wilkin* (1967) ECR 407, if there are several agreements which when added together do have a significant effect, then they will breach Article 81.

In order for something to satisfy this aspect of Article 81, it must either have:

▌ a direct or indirect effect on trade between Member States; or
▌ the capability of such an effect.

This is a very wide definition, and is made wider still by the fact that the term 'trade' is also given a very wide meaning, but importantly, if it doesn't affect trade between Member States, then it should be dealt with by national law, and not EU law.

# Exemptions from Article 81

It is possible for an agreement under Article 81 not to be declared void if it fulfils *all* of the following conditions:

▌ It contributes to improving production or distribution of goods or to promoting technical or economic progress
▌ It allows consumers a fair share of this benefit
▌ It does not impose conditions that are not necessary to achieve the above
▌ It does not allow undertakings to eliminate a substantial amount of competition.

# Application of exemptions

There were previously three ways of gaining an exemption:

| Method of exemption | Explanation |
| --- | --- |
| Individual exemption | Application to the Commission for a decision as to whether the agreement falls within Article 81(3). This has now been removed by Regulation 1/2003 |
| Comfort letter | An alternative to the individual decision, this is an informal opinion from the Commission that the agreement does not breach Article 81. Saves time, but is non-binding and has no legal effect. Also now essentially defunct |
| Block exemption | Blanket exemptions in certain industries passed by regulation. Again, this saves Commission time, by allowing blanket exemption in industries where it is recognised that the majority of agreements should be exempted, for example certain types of vertical agreements |

## FURTHER THINKING: REGULATION 1/2003

This regulation changed the existing system of individual notification and comfort letters. These procedures took a lot of the Commission's time, and so the regulation devolved the matter down to national level. This was done by making Article 81(3) directly effective, and so it allowed companies themselves to resolve any problems in *national* courts of Member States. Cases decided under the old system are still relevant, and can still be used in answering assessment questions in this area. The new system was brought into force on 1 May 2004, in time for the accession of ten new states – if it had not taken effect, then the Commission would probably have been completely overloaded with work from the new Member States.

The only drawback is that it has removed the comfort previously given by the Commission taking responsibility for this area. However, it has allowed national courts to deal with these matters.

See Roitman, D. (2006) 'Legal Uncertainty for Vertical Distribution Agreements: The Block Exemption Regulation 2790/1999 (BER) and Related Aspects of the New Regulation 1/2003'

Saunders, O.O.R. (2006) 'Regulation 1/2003 – An Effective Mechanism for Managing Economic and Monetary Union in an Enlarged Community?'

Venit, J.S. (2003) 'Brave New World: The Modernisation and Decentralisation of Enforcement under Articles 81 and 82 of the EC Treaty'

**EXAM TIP**

Although Article 81 presents itself as a list of criteria to fulfil, it is still important to make sure you are able to discuss examples from the cases. Examiners will be looking for depth of knowledge, and the amount you understand of how Article 81 operates will come through in your answer.

# Article 82: abuse of a dominant position

**KEY STATUTE**

### Article 82(1)

Any abuse by one or more undertakings of a dominant position within the common market or in a substantial part of it shall be prohibited as incompatible with the common market in so far as it may affect trade between Member States.

Unlike Article 81, Article 82 tends to involve just one company abusing a strong position in the marketplace that they are working in. (It can involve several companies working together to produce a combined dominance.) Therefore, in order to deal with this area, you need to define several important elements. Article 82 just requires:

- An undertaking (see the definition under Article 81)
- A dominant position
- Abuse of that dominant position
- Effect on trade between Member States.

If all of these elements are present, then there is a breach of Article 82.

# Market dominance

**Case 27/76** *United Brands* v. *Commission* **(1978) ECR 207**

**Concerning: definition of a dominant position**

**Facts**

United Brands were importers of bananas. They imposed various terms on the companies they supplied, for example insisting that bananas were not sold while still green, charging different prices to different suppliers in different countries, and in some circumstances, refusing to supply bananas. They were accused by the Commission of abusing a dominant position in their market.

**Legal principle**

A dominant position was defined as being a position of economic strength which allowed two things: (i) the dominant undertaking to *hinder effective competition*, and (ii) the undertaking to *act independently* of its competitors and consumers.

In order to establish this dominance, it is important to look at the relevant market. For example, in *United Brands*, the court had to decide whether the relevant market was for bananas or more generally for fruit. To establish what the market is, you need to look at the following:

| Market | Explanation |
| --- | --- |
| Relevant product market (RPM) | Two important factors: the ability to substitute your product for other similar products, and the similarity of your products to other products |
| Geographical market | You need to consider how large a geographical area the company operates in. It must be 'the common market or a substantial part of it' |

These issues then feed into a consideration of how dominant the undertaking is. For example:

Case 27/76 *United Brands* v. *Commission*: United Brands were dominant because the RPM was 'bananas', and not more generally 'fruit'. Bananas were different enough from other fruit for them not to be cross-substitutable.

Case T-83/91 *Tetra-Pak* v. *Commission* (1994) ECR II-755: The relevant geographical market was the whole of the EU.

*B&I Line* v. *Sealink Harbours & Stena Sealink* (1992) 5 CMLR 255: Because the market concerned the control of harbours (rather limited because of the number of harbours in the EU) then a single harbour was a substantial part of the geographical market.

These factors then feed into the issue of dominance as a fact. Here are some examples:

| Case | Situation of dominance |
| --- | --- |
| Case 85/76 *Hoffman la Roche* v. *Commission* (1979) ECR 1869 | 70–80% share in the market |
| Case 27/76 *United Brands* v. *Commission* (1978) ECR 207 | 40–45% share in the market |
| Case T-219/99 *British Airways* v. *Commission* (2004) All ER (EC) 1115 | 39.7% share in the market, where the nearest competitor, Virgin, had 5.5% share |

### EXAM TIP

Dominance can be relative, as shown by the *British Airways* case in the table above. BA had less than half the share in its market that Hoffman la Roche did in their case, but because BA's nearest rival had a much smaller share, they were still dominant. Think when you consider if an undertaking is dominant, rather than just seeing if they have the majority (over 50%) of the market.

# Abuse

Dominance on its own is ***not*** a breach of Article 82. However, the abuse of that dominant position is. There is a non-exclusive list in Article 82 of examples:

### KEY STATUTE

### Article 82(2)

Such abuse may, in particular, consist in:

(a) directly or indirectly imposing unfair purchase or selling prices or other unfair trading conditions;

(b) limiting production, markets or technical development to the prejudice of consumers;

(c) applying dissimilar conditions to equivalent transactions with other trading parties, thereby placing them at a competitive disadvantage;

(d) making the conclusion of contracts subject to acceptance by the other parties of supplementary obligations which, by their nature or according to commercial usage, have no connection with the subject of such contracts.

The *United Brands* case is such a good case to apply here, because they were actually doing all four of the things listed above! There are other examples, though, and some of these have been listed below:

| Case | Abuse |
|---|---|
| Case 226/84 *British Leyland* v. *Commission* (1986) ECR 3263 | Unfair prices: charging more for approval certificates for left hand drive cars |
| Case 238/87 *Volvo* v. *Eric Veng* (1988) ECR 6211 | Limiting the market: use of intellectual property rights to prevent competitors from producing spare parts for Volvo cars |
| Case T-219/99 *British Airways* v. *Commission* (2004) All ER (EC) 1115 | Discrimination: use of a dominant position in the market for travel agents to discriminate between levels of commission paid to agents |
| Case 85/76 *Hoffman la Roche* v. *Commission* (1979) ECR 1869 | Tying in: a tying in clause stopped suppliers from buying from Hoffman's competitors, and allowed them to control the market |
| Case T-70/89 *Radio Telefis Eireann* v. *Commission* (1991) ECR II-485 | Refusal to supply: RTE and BBC refused to license TV listings information to competitors, therefore preventing competition for TV listings magazines |

### FURTHER THINKING: 'ESSENTIAL FACILITIES'?

The *RTE* case above seems to have led to an 'essential facilities doctrine', where if an undertaking refuses to license or supply (on reasonable terms) something which is considered an 'essential facility', then this can also be an abuse. This has a particular effect on those companies that produce things which cannot be reproduced by their competitors. This appears to put a higher level of control on companies that are in this position. Bear this in mind if dealing with a problem question that appears to involve a company that makes something that their competitors cannot make themselves.

See Stothers, C. (2001) 'Refusal to Supply as Abuse of a Dominant Position: the Essential Facilities Doctrine in the European Union'.

# Effect on trade between Member States

The effect of a breach on trade between Member States seems to have been very widely construed, as with Article 81, to prevent it obstructing the use of Article 82. Any effect on the market between Member States is enough.

**EXAM TIP**

The issues of the market and whether a company is dominant or not are ones to be dealt with on an individual basis, so it is important for you to be able to *apply* the law rather than just present the criteria in your answer.

# Chapter summary:
# **Putting it all together**

## TEST YOURSELF

☐ Can you tick all the points from the revision checklist at the beginning of this chapter?

☐ Take the **end-of-chapter quiz** on the companion website.

☐ Test your knowledge of the cases below with the **revision flashcards** on the website.

☐ Attempt the essay question from the beginning of the chapter using the guidelines below.

☐ Go to the companion website to try out other questions.

## Answer guidelines

**See the essay question at the start of the chapter.**

The question itself appears to be very specific in its focus, but don't let this mislead you. A wider appreciation of Article 81 and how it operates will also need to be discussed in order to allow you to evaluate how Regulation 1/2003 has affected the way in which it works. You will need to discuss:

- The requirements of Article 81, in particular the criteria for breach of this Article
- The type of agreements considered to breach Article 81
- The exceptions listed under Article 81(3)
- Examples of how these have been applied under the previous system of comfort letters and individual notification
- The consequences of removing control over Article 81 from the Commission – see Regulation 1/2003.

**Make your answer stand out**
The temptation here will be merely to follow the flow diagram provided in this chapter and take a 'write everything you know about' approach to answering this question. However, this will not address the core of what this question is asking you, and therefore you need to think about how the working knowledge you have of Article 81 allows you to produce an informed answer to the question.

## FURTHER READING

Korah, V. (1980) 'Concept of a Dominant Position Within the Meaning of Article 86', 17 CML Rev 395

Roitman, D. (2006) 'Legal Uncertainty for Vertical Distribution Agreements: The Block Exemption Regulation 2790/1999 (BER) and Related Aspects of the New Regulation 1/2003', 27 ECLR 261

Saunders, O.O.R. (2006) 'Regulation 1/2003 – An Effective Mechanism for Managing Economic and Monetary Union in an Enlarged Community?', 27 Business Law Review 148

Stothers, C. (2001) 'Refusal to Supply as Abuse of a Dominant Position: the Essential Facilities Doctrine in the European Union', 22(7) ECLR 256

Venit, J.S. (2003) 'Brave New World: The Modernisation and Decentralisation of Enforcement under Articles 81 and 82 of the EC Treaty', 40 CMLR 545

Vogelaar, F. (2005) 'European Competition Law Revisited: the "Great Overhaul" of 2004 Analysed', 32 Legal IEI 105

# And finally, before the exam . . .

By using this book to direct your revision, you should now have a good grasp of the way in which the EU operates, and the key areas of substantive law. Remember that the information contained in this guide is not intended to substitute for your own notes and textbook reading, but to help to point you in the right direction when using these sources, which are going to have much more depth and detail than can be included here. Most importantly, you should check to make sure you have *understood* the different topic areas here, as this will be crucial to success. EU law requires you to understand how the system operates as well as how the law is applied.

| TEST YOURSELF |
|---|
| ☐ Look at the revision checklists at the start of each chapter. Are you happy that you can now tick them all? If not, go back to the particular chapter and work through the material again. If you are still struggling, **seek help** from your tutor. |
| ☐ Go to the companion website and revisit the interactive **quizzes** provided for each chapter. |
| ☐ Make sure you can recall the **legal principles** of the key cases and statutes which you have revised. |
| ☐ Go to the companion website and test your knowledge of cases and terms with the **revision flashcards.** |
| ☐ Ensure you have understood the procedures as well as the principles behind the subjects: because EU law uses different procedure from UK law, it may be easy to get confused otherwise. |

☐ If you are having problems with case names, remember that they are often abbreviated in a common way by all textbook writers and lecturers: e.g. *R v Secretary of State for Transport ex parte Factortame* is commonly just referred to as '*Factortame*'.

☐ If you are allowed to take a statute book in to the exam, make sure you are familiar with the EC Treaty, and its numbering. All Articles relating to a particular subject tend to be grouped together: for example all powers of the European Commission are contained in Articles 211–219, and all Articles relating to the free movement of goods and customs union are in Articles 23–31.

# Linking it all up

Check where there are overlaps between subject areas. Make a careful note of these as a knowledge of how one topic can lead into another can increase your marks significantly.

There can be overlap in a question between a procedural area and a substantive area, for example:

▪ Between one of the free movement areas and Article 226, because this question will be about both the law itself and the action that can be taken to enforce that law.

▪ Sources of law areas can overlap with Article 234 (interpretation by the ECJ), because this will concern the way in which an individual may be able to enforce law in national courts.

▪ Questions concerning the powers of the Institutions can overlap with specific procedures that may be used by those Institutions – for example, Article 230 (Judicial Review) is a specific example of how any of the primary Institutions can exercise their powers to supervise the other Institutions' activities.

## Essay Question

On 1 March 1999 the European Commission resigned to avoid the European Parliament exercising its power of censure against it. This power is a key aspect of the checks and balances system that has been developing at EU level with the changes made by Treaties over the past 30 years. Discuss this system and evaluate how satisfactory it is at monitoring the activity within the EU.

# Answer guidelines

This question is designed to pull in several subjects and test your ability to draw links between the different areas of EU law in a discussion of the system. It is focused upon the supervisory powers of the Institutions, but in order to fully answer the question, you also need to make sure that other overlapping areas are also covered. The following are issues you will need to consider in dealing with this question:

▐ The system the question mentions has developed with changes made by the Single European Act, the Maastricht Treaty, the Treaty of Amsterdam, and the Treaty of Nice.

▐ Specific examples from the above Treaties focus on the powers of the Parliament, so discuss their powers of supervision and censure over the Commission, and possible reasons behind it, and their powers to monitor the Council of Ministers through questioning.

▐ The Council of Ministers also has supervisory powers, for example, their power of appointment of the Commission.

▐ The increased involvement of the Parliament in making law has allowed it to have a greater say in the law making process, so you can discuss the procedures of cooperation and co-decision here.

▐ Articles 230 and 232 (Judicial Review) allow any of the Institutions to challenge improper procedural actions under the Treaty and also form part of the system of checks and balances. The grounds for challenge are relevant here, and therefore it will allow you to evaluate how effective this is as part of the system of checks and balances.

▐ Your evaluation of the EU system will dictate the answer you produce – but it is worth bearing in mind that although this is a question which covers several areas, you should remain focused upon the question. This is **not** about writing everything you know about this area – it requires a critical discussion.

# Glossary of terms

The glossary is divided into two parts: **key definitions** and **other useful terms**. The **key definitions** can be found within the chapter in which they occur as well as at the end of the book. These definitions are the essential terms that you must know and understand in order to prepare for an exam.

The additional list, **other useful terms** provides further definitions of useful terms and phrases which will also help you answer examination and coursework questions effectively. These terms are highlighted in the text as they occur but the definition can only be found here.

## ■ Key definitions

| | |
|---|---|
| *Acte clair* | A condition under which an issue of EU law is clear and does not need to be clarified by the ECJ |
| Court of last instance | In a court structure, this is the very last or highest court that a particular case can reach |
| Court or tribunal | Generally a court or tribunal is one that has a judicial function, and independence from the parties concerned |
| Derogation | The exemption from, or the relaxation of, a particular law |
| Dualist | A dualist legal system is one where international agreements also have to be passed by the national parliament |
| Goods | Goods are interpreted as 'products which can be valued in money and which are capable, as such, of forming the subject of commercial transactions'. (Case 7/68 *Re Export Tax on Art Treasures: EC Commission* v. *Italy* (1968) ECR 423 at 428) |
| Horizontal effect | A piece of EU legislation has horizontal effect where it is enforceable by an individual against another individual |
| Indistinctly applicable measures | These are restrictions or other measures which apply equally to imported products and domestic products |
| Legislative power | The power of the Institutions to make law |

| | |
|---|---|
| **Making a reference** | Under Article 234, where a national court sends questions to the ECJ for interpretation |
| **Negative duty** | A duty not to do something |
| **Qualified Majority Voting** | Qualified Majority Voting is a form of voting where a certain percentage of the total vote must be in favour, usually around two thirds of the vote |
| **Reasoned opinion** | Under Article 226, the reasoned opinion is a written statement from the Commission which lays down the obligation concerned, and the reasons why the Member State has failed to meet this obligation. It should clearly spell out the Commission's objection, and therefore it should be possible for the Member State to know what it needs to do to rectify this |
| **Supervisory power** | The power of the Institutions to supervise each other |
| **Undertakings** | This is intended to cover only private individuals, and so it means natural persons (such as you and I) or legal persons (companies). However, in the context of Article 81, it has also been defined as groups of companies too |
| **Vertical effect** | A piece of EU legislation has vertical effect where it is enforceable by an individual against the State |
| **Worker** | A worker is an EU national who is either in employment (full or part time) in that he/she is paid in return for his/her performance under an employer/employee relationship, or is seeking actual paid work |

# Other useful terms

| | |
|---|---|
| **Acquis communitaire** | The existing body of EU law, all cases and legislation, both primary and secondary |
| **Adversarial** | A procedure where the parties concerned present their own evidence and the court decides the case based upon this |
| **Community Act** | Any legislation made under EU law, whether Treaties or secondary legislation under Article 249 |
| *Locus standi* | A condition under which an individual or other entity has the permission or status to bring a case before the ECJ |
| **MEQR** | Measures equivalent to quantitative restrictions |
| **Primary legislation** | In the EU context, this is Treaty law agreed by the Member States |
| **Secondary legislation** | Law made by the Institutions under the powers given to them in Article 249 |

# Index

Emboldened page references
indicates that the entry appears
in the glossary

abuse of a dominant position,
Art.82
  abuse 113
    Art.82(2) provisions 115
    'essential facilities doctrine'
      116
    examples 116
  application, 105, 113
    Art. 82(1) provisions 113
  dominant position 113
    acting independently 114
    definition, *United Brands*
      114, 116
    examples 114–15
    hindering effective
      competition 114
    relevant market,
      establishing 114
    effect on Member States' trade
      113, 117
  'essential facilities doctrine' 116
  undertaking, 113, **124**
adversarial, definition **124**
anti-competitive agreement,
  Art.81
  application of 105, 107, 108–9
  Art. 81(1) and (2), provisions
    106
  *de minimus* and 111
  effect on trade between
    Member States 111
  exemptions
    application of 111–12, 118
    block exemptions 112
    comfort letter 112
    conditions avoiding void
      agreements 111
    devolution to national
      courts 112, 118
  object or effect of restricting
    competition

horizontal agreements 109,
  **123**
object or effect, either 109
relevant market, within 109
types of agreement 109,
  110, 118
vertical agreements 109,
  **124**
prohibitions
  categories 108
  'concerted practice'
    meaning 108, 109
    examples 110
  restrictive practices check
    chart 107
  undertakings, definition 107–
    8, **124**

competition law
  context and prohibitions 105
  *see also* abuse of a dominant
    position, Art.82;
    anti-competitive agreement,
    Art.81

enforcement actions against
    Member States
  action by the Commission
    administrative stage 35–6,
      41
    Art. 226 provision 34
    Commission discretion 36,
      42
    Court finding and State
      compliance 37
    failure to fulfill an obligation
      34
    judicial stage 37, 41
    procedure 34–5
    reasoned opinion, 35, 36,
      37, **124**
  action by Member State
    Art.227 provision 36, 37, 41
    problems with 39
    procedure 38

Direct Effects, Doctrine of 8–9,
  34
  enforcement factors and
    procedure 39
  Free Movement of Goods and
    41
  interim orders 39–40
  purpose of Arts. 226–8
    enforcement system,
      elements in 33–4
    procedure 33–4
    reason for 32
  remedies, other 39–40
  state liability, non-
    implementation, 12–
    13, 34

Free Movement of goods
  basic provision under Art.23 75
  *Cassis*, indirectly applicable
    measure, Art.28
    case details and decision 79
    first *Cassis* rule, Rule of
      Reason 80
    second *Cassis* rule, mutual
      recognition 81
  Customs union, Art. 25
    imposition of additional
      duty, decision 77
    negative duty, definition 76,
      **124**
    negative duty not to impose
      duties 76
  derogations from Arts. 28 and
    29
    Art.30 justification
      provisions 85
    justification, examples from
      cases 86
    non-exhaustive list of
      situations 85
  EC Treaty and principle of 28–
    30, 74, 75, 76
  enforcement actions and
    Member States 41

Free Movement of goods
(*continued*)
goods, definition 76, **123**
indistinctly applicable
measures
*Cassis*, validity of under
Art.28 79–81, 87
definition 79, **123**
liberalisation of Art.28 and
indistinctly applicable
measures
selling arrangement
measure *Keck* 82, 87
selling arrangement and
other deals 82
main provisions, Arts.25, 28–
30 76
measures equivalent to effect
to quantitative
restrictions (MEQRs)
definition 78, **124**
distinctly applicable
measures 78, 79
indistinctly applicable
measures 78, 79–81
restrictions on exports, Art.29
Art.29 provisions 83
flow chart 84
restriction of internal EU
trade, objective 85
restrictions on imports, Art.28
Art.28 provisions 77
duty to take positive action
77
MEQRs 77, 78–83
quantitative restrictions 77,
78
Free movement of workers
Art.39 provisions, key
elements 91–2
basic EU right linking other
freedoms 90, 102
derogations from
circumstances allowing
98–9
conduct of the person
99–100
derogation definition 98,
**123**
public health 101
public policy, examples of
cases 99–100

public policy meaning,
examples 98
public policy and public
security 98–9, 100
rights of family members and
dependents children 97
entitlement under Directive
2004/38 97
rights of a worker
Art. 39(3), Treaty provisions
95
non-discrimination under
Art, 39(3) 96
public sector work 96
sources of 96
secondary legislation, under
economic examples of
'worker' 93
formal aspects of 'worker'
94
worker, definition and
examples 92–3, **124**
working and seeking work
94–5
working and seeking work
limited period as worker
upon arrival 94
limited period with
employment chance 95

Institutions of the EU
Committee of the Regions 22
Council the European Union
(Council of Ministers)
composition 20
European Council,
distinguished 21, 23
functions 18
Presidency of 20–1
qualified majority voting 20,
**124**
Court of Auditors 22, 47
Economic and Social
Committee 22
European Commission,
composition 19, 21
European Court of Justice and
Court of First Instance
composition 21–2
European Court on Human
Rights, distinguished
from 22, 26

precedent, problem area 26
role 19, 25–6
European Parliament 18
composition and functions
19
legislative procedure 24
Privileged Applicant status
47
functions of 17
'institutional balance' 18
other Institutions 22
political influences between
the Institutions 28
relationships between
Institutions 24, 26–7
supervisory powers 23, 24–5,
**124**
Institutions of the EU, powers
legislative powers
definition 23, **123**
European Parliament,
procedure 24
relationships between
Institutions 24, 26–7,
29
powers and duties of each 23
supervisory power
definition 23, **124**
overview of powers 24–5, 29

judicial review, Arts 230 and 232
annulment of a Community act
45, **124**
consequences, compliance
with judgment 53
direct and individual concern
to the person
direct concern 50
examples of 49
fixed closed class 50, 54
test for 49
time limit 50
failure to act, action for,
Art.232
individual challenges 52
institution defines its
position 52
*locus standi* 51, **124**
non-privileged applicants 52
procedure 52–3
reviewable omissions 52
unity principle 51, 53

*locus standi*, ability to
  challenge act, Art.230
  categories and scope 46, 48
  direct and individual
    concern to the person
    49–51
  equivalent to a decision,
    individuals and 48
  non-privileged applicants,
    Art.230 48
  private persons and
    companies 48
  privileged applicants 46, 47
  regulation, equivalent to a
    decision 48–9
  privileged applicants, Art.230
    category and scope 46–7
    European Parliament and 47
  procedure, Art.230 44, 45
  reasons to challenge
    Community Act, 51
  reviewable acts 45
  secondary sources, limitation
    to 46
  semi-privileged applicants,
    Art.230 46, 47
  time limit 50

legislation, forms of EU
  Community act **124**
  Decisions 4, 10, 14
  Directions 4
  Directives 4, 10, 12–13, 14
  primary legislation 3–4, **124**
  Regulations 4, 10, 14
  Regulations and Opinions 4
  secondary legislation 4, **124**
  treaties 3–4, 10, 14

preliminary rulings, European
  Court of Justice
  Art.234
  *Acte Clair* principle
    definition 68, **123**
    example cases 68–9
    overlap with CILFIT criteria
    69

European Court of Justice,
  powers of
  interpretation role, not
    decisions 62
  jurisdiction over questions
    raised 60–1
  national courts, boundary
    between 61
European Court of Justice, role
  of 60
  interpretation, consistency in
    57, 58, 71
national court compulsory
  references
  *Acte Clair* principle 68–9, **123**
  circumstances when not
    necessary 67
  court of last instance,
    concrete and
    abstract theory 66–7
  court of last instance,
    definition 66, **123**
  exception to, CILFIT
    principle 58, 67, 69
  making a reference,
    definition 66, **123**
  provisions on 65
national court discretion to
  refer
  appropriateness of
    references 65
  provisions on 64–5
procedure, provisions 59, 71
references, courts eligible to
  make
  arbitrators 64
  court or tribunal, meaning
    62–3, **123**
  domestic tribunals 64
  Dutch medical association
    63
  exclusions 64
  scope of 57

sources and application of EU
  law
  *acquis communitaire* 2, **124**

direct applicability and direct
  effects
  direct effect, criteria for 9
  direct enforcement 8, 34
  directives, direct effect and
    10–11
  general definitions 7–8
  'state, the', meaning 10–11,
    14
  treaties, 7, 10
  types of Community law,
    effect on 10
  vertical and horizontal effect
    9–10, 109, **123**, **124**
forms of legislation 3–4
other ways of enforcement in
  national courts
  indirect effect 11–12
  interpretation obligation,
    'von Colson principle'
    12
  non-implementation, state
    liability 12–13, 34
  state liability, conditions for,
    *Francovich* 13
primary legislation 3–4
secondary legislation 4
supremacy of EU law 2, 5–7
supremacy of EU law 2
  conflicting national law,
    *Factortame* 7
  dualist legal system 5, **123**
  inconsistent laws, dealing with
    5–7
  Member States and 2, 5
  Parliamentary Supremacy,
    Doctrine of 5
  United Kingdom, effect on 6

Treaties, EU
  direct applicability, 7, 10
  order of 4
  range of 3
  Treaty article renumbering 60,
    77
  vertical and horizontal effect
    10

# The essential reference for all students of law

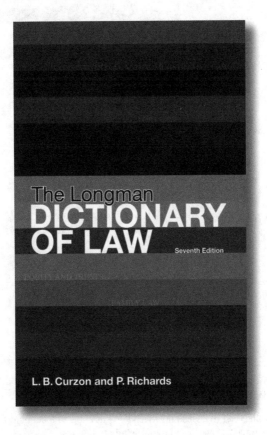

- Fully comprehensive entries on all aspects of English Law
- Clear definitions of specialised legal terminology
- Cross-referenced, giving full references for cases and statutes

The dictionary is fully supported by a companion website which links to additional legal information and provides updates to definitions.

Available from all good bookshops or order online at:

**www.pearsoned.co.uk/law**

EU LAW

Visit the Law Express Series Companion Website at **www.pearsoned.co.uk/lawexpress**
to find valuable **student** learning material including:

▪ A study plan test to assess how well you know the subject before you begin your
revision, now broken down into targeted study units

▪ Interactive quizzes with a variety of question types to test your knowledge of the
main points from each chapter of the book

▪ Further examination questions and guidelines for answering them

▪ Interactive flashcards to help you revise the main terms and cases

▪ Printable versions of the topic maps and checklists

Plus:

▪ 'You be the marker' allows you to see exam questions and answers from the
perspective of the examiner and includes notes on how an answer might be marked

▪ Podcasts prov                                                    non exam
question

9030 00000 0412 3